The Study and Teaching of Anthropology

Pertti J. Pelto

University of Connecticut

Raymond H. Muessig

The Ohio State University

Charles E. Merrill Publishing Company
A Bell & Howell Company
Columbus   Toronto   London   Sydney

The Study and Teaching of Social Science Series
Raymond H. Muessig, Editor

Published by Charles E. Merrill Publishing Co.
A Bell & Howell Company
Columbus, Ohio 43216

This book was set in Souvenir
Cover Design Coordination: Will Chenoweth
Production Coordination: Linda Hillis Bayma

Credits: Specific acknowledgments of permissions to use materials appear on page iv, which is to be considered an extension of this copyright page. Standard credit and source information appears in the *Notes*.

Photos: Cover by Jose Bermuez; Instituto Nacional de Antropologia e Historia, 33; Gretal H. Pelto, 40, 63 (top); Pertti J. Pelto, 24, 25, 38, 54, 60, 61, 63 (bottom), 65, 67, 73, 75 (top); L. Müller Wille, 75 (bottom).

Library of Congress Catalog Card Number: 79-90157
International Standard Book Number: 0-675-08192-0

1 2 3 4 5 6 7 8 9 10—85 84 83 82 81 80

Printed in the United States of America

To the memory of
Jaakko Pelto

Acknowledgments

From THE GOLDEN PENINSULA: CULTURE AND ADAPTATION IN MAINLAND SOUTHEAST ASIA by Charles F. Keyes. Copyright 1977 by Macmillan Publishing Co., Inc. Reprinted by permission of Macmillan Publishing Co., Inc.

Excerpt from CHARLOTTE'S WEB by E.B. White. Copyright, 1952, by E.B. White. By permission of Harper & Row, Publishers, Inc.

Reprinted by permission of Athenum Publishers from MRS. FRISBY AND THE RATS OF NIMH by Robert C. O'Brien. Copyright ©1971 Robert C. O'Brien.

From WATERSHIP DOWN by Richard Adams. Copyright 1972 by Macmillan Publishing Co., Inc. Reprinted by permission of Macmillan Publishing Co., Inc.

Excerpts from JULIE OF THE WOLVES by Jean Craighead George. Text copyright ©1972 by Jean Craighead George. By permission of Harper & Row, Publishers, Inc.

From GENTLE BEN by Walt Morey. Copyright, ©1965 by Walt Morey. Reprinted by permission of the publishers, Elseview-Dutton.

Copyright ©1971 by Allan W. Eckert. From INCIDENT AT HAWK'S HILL by Allan W. Eckert, by permission of Little, Brown and Co. in association with the Atlantic Monthly Press.

From GIFTS OF AN EAGLE by Kent Durden. Copyright ©1972 by Kent Durden. Reprinted by permission of SIMON & SCHUSTER, A Division of Gulf & Western Corporation.

Copyright ©1963 by Farley Mowat. From NEVER CRY WOLF by Farley Mowat, by permission of Little, Brown and Co. in association with the Atlantic Monthly Press.

From IN THE SHADOW OF MAN by Jane van Lawick-Goodall. Copyright 1971 by Houghton Mifflin Company. Reprinted by permission of Houghton Mifflin Company.

From LUCY: GROWING UP HUMAN by Maurice Temerlin. Copyright 1977 by Science and Behavior Books, Inc. Reprinted by permission of Science and Behavior Books, Inc.

From THE OFFICIAL CB SLANGUAGE LANGUAGE DICTIONARY by Lanie Dills. Copyright 1976 by Louis J. Martin & Associates, Inc. Reprinted by permission of Louis J. Martin & Associates, Inc.

From VIVENT LES DIFFERENCES: AN INTERMEDIATE READER FOR COMMUNICATION by Gilbert A. Jarvis, Therese M. Bonin, Donald E. Corbin, and Diane W. Birckbichler. Copyright ©1977 by Holt, Rinehart and Winston. Reprinted by permission of Holt, Rinehart and Winston.

From JI NONGO NONGO MEANS RIDDLES BY Verna Aardema, text copyright ©1978 by Verna Aardema. Reprinted by permission of Four Winds Press, a division of Scholastic Magazines, Inc.

From HAUSA FOLKLORE, CUSTOMS, PROVERBS, ETC., VOLUME II by Robert S. Rattray. Copyright by Oxford at the Clarendon Press. Reprinted by permission of Clarendon Press.

From THE MAASAI by S. S. Sankan. Copyright 1971 by The English Press. Reprinted by permission of the Ministry of Education, Kenya Literature Bureau, Nairobi, Kenya.

From MIRACLES by Richard Lewis. Copyright ©1966 by Richard Lewis. Reprinted by permission of SIMON & SCHUSTER, a Division of Gulf & Western Corporation.

From SCOOUWA: JAMES SMITH'S INDIAN CAPTIVITY NARRATIVE by John J. Barsotti. Copyright 1978 by The Ohio Historical Society. Reprinted by permission of the Ohio Historical Society.

From ANTHROPOLOGISTS IN CITIES by George M. Foster and Robert V. Kemper. Published in 1974 by Little, Brown & Co. Reprinted by permission of George M. Foster.

From THE PAST IS HUMAN by Peter White (Taplinger, 1976). ©1974 by Peter White. Reprinted by permission.

From "The First Emperor's Army: China's Incredible Find" *National Geographic* 153, no. 4 (April 1978). Reprinted by permission of *National Geographic*.

Excerpted from IN SMALL THINGS FORGOTTEN, by James Deetz. Copyright ©1977 by James Deetz. Reprinted by permission of Doubleday & Company, Inc.

From THE GENTLE TASADAY by John Nance. Copyright 1975 by Harcourt Brace Jovanovich, Inc. Reprinted by permission of Harcourt Brace Jovanovich, Inc.

Foreword

The Study and Teaching of Social Science Series is composed of six books, *The Study and Teaching of Anthropology, The Study and Teaching of Economics, The Study and Teaching of Geography, The Study and Teaching of History, The Study and Teaching of Political Science,* and *The Study and Teaching of Sociology.* In the larger part of every one of the six volumes, the social scientist was asked to deal with the nature and development of his field, goals of and purposes served by the discipline, tools and procedures employed by scholars, significant and helpful literature in the field, and fundamental questions asked and ideas generated by the academic area. Writers were challenged not only to provide solid subject matter but also to treat content in a clear, concise, interesting, useful manner.

Each of the six works in the series concludes with a chapter entitled "Suggested Methods for Teachers," which was written after reading and considering the complete manuscript by the individual social scientist.

In a number of ways, *The Study and Teaching of Social Science Series* resembles *The Social Science Seminar Series* (published in 1965) from which it is descended. The idea for *The Social Science Seminar Series* came to me in 1963, when the structure-of-the-disciplines approach in social studies education was receiving considerable attention in publications, meetings, and projects. At that time, social studies educators and supervisors and others were searching for substantive material concerned with the essence of academic disciplines and for down-to-earth ideas for specific classroom learning activities. They sought materials which would spell out and facilitate ways of translating abstract social science concepts and generalizations into concrete inquiry strategies that would be meaningful and appealing to children and youth. In the early sixties, some historians, economists, sociologists, anthropologists, political scientists, and geographers were trying to think of ways that others could teach respectable social science to elementary and secondary students about whom the academicians had little knowledge and with whom university scholars had no experience. And certain classroom teachers and others in professional education were informed with respect to human growth and development, child and adolescent psychology, theories of instruction in general and of social studies education in particular, day-to-day classroom organization and management, etcetera, and could work and relate well with younger pupils. These practitioners, however, readily admitted their lack of the kind of breadth and depth in all of the various social sciences necessary to do even an adequate job of defining and interpreting the disciplines. They frequently added that they had insufficient financial resources, time, energy, background in methods and media, creativity, and writing talent to produce for themselves and others the pages of requisite, appropriate, fresh, variegated, pedagogical alternatives needed to reach heterogeneous collections of learners at all instructional levels.

Thus, it seemed to me that a very real need could be met be a series of solid, practical, readable books where the content on each discipline would be written by a specialist in that social science and where the material on teaching strategies would be developed by a specialist in social studies education.

Now, some brief comments are appropriate regarding the revised and many completely new approaches for the last chapters in *The Study and Teaching of Social Science Series.*

The 1965 *Social Science Seminar Series* was designed primarily to assist K-12 teachers in the application of a structure-of-the-disciplines social studies theory in their classrooms. Since the needs and pursuits of the many users of the series have changed and become more diverse than they were in 1965, and since I, too, have changed in the ensuing years, this 1980 rendering is considerably more eclectic than its progenitor. Rarely is there a one-to-one relationship between a specific teaching method and a particular, overall theory of social studies education. Additionally, a myriad of instructional media may be matched with different philosophies and techniques. And, a single theory of social studies education need not be followed by an entire school district, by a whole school, by all of the teachers at the same grade level, or even by a given teacher throughout a school year with each of the students. The suggested methods in the last chapters of *The Study and Teaching of Social Science Series,* then, can be used as presented, modified to suit various classroom situations, adapted to complement different social studies theories, and altered to fit numerous goals and objectives. In the final analysis, a key test of a teaching method is the extent to which it touches the life of an individual learner in a meaningful way.

A Special Acknowledgment

When Charles E. Merrill Publishing Company expressed an interest in my plan to develop a series of texts in social science and invited me to submit a detailed proposal, I immediately asked Dr. Vincent R. Rogers (then at the University of Minnesota and now at the University of Connecticut) if he would join me as co-editor of the series and co-author of the chapters on instructional approaches. I worked with Professor Rogers on the refined plan that was sent to and approved by Merrill. Vin Rogers and I had written together previously in an easy, relaxed, compatible, mutually advantageous manner. We were both former classroom teachers who had become university professors of social studies education. We shared a feeling for the needs, interests, problems, and aspirations of students and teachers, had a serious commitment to the social sciences, and were familiar with a variety of instructional media. But, more than any other person I could find and attract as a co-worker on the endeavor, Rogers could translate significant ideas into functional, sequential, additive, meaningful, imaginative, enjoyable methods. Vin did his share throughout the entire undertaking, and he was responsible for the securing of all but one of the initial social science authors of the first version of this program. Our writing together on *The*

Social Science Seminar Series went swimmingly, and we emerged even better friends than before.

When Merrill requested that Dr. Rogers and I revise and create new material for our concluding chapters for the six books in *The Study and Teaching of Social Science Series,* I anticipated the pleasure of a collaboration again. However, Professor Rogers already had too many previous commitments to undertake something as time consuming and demanding as this effort, and he had to withdraw, unfortunately. True to his generous personal and professional nature, Professor Rogers told me to use any or all of the ideas he and I had developed separately and together about fifteen years ago. We blended so well in the sixties, and so many things have happened since that time, that I doubt whether I could easily distinguish between our original suggestions anyway. Thus, my sincere thanks to Vin for his contribution to the first series and to this second undertaking.

Raymond H. Muessig

Preface

In the fifteen years since I wrote the first edition of *The Study of Anthropology* we humans have experienced the agonies of the Vietnam War, at least two periods of energy crisis, and the excitement of putting a man on the moon. In the same period SSTs came into regular use, a worldwide ecology movement took shape, and hypertension and heart disease became popular concerns. The spectors of polio epidemics and smallpox outbreaks faded into oblivion.

Meanwhile, anthropologists and other scientists found new fossil evidence (mainly in E. Africa) that pushed back our estimates of "earliest human-kind" at least another million or more years.

Methods of anthropological research have developed a good deal during this past decade-and-a-half, especially in the extent to which researchers now make use of more systematic data-gathering tools and statistical procedures. Many new lines of anthropological specialization have developed, including exciting new research in medical anthropology, legal anthropology, and anthropology-in-education.

In the face of great changes in the human condition over the past fifteen years, and the accumulation of great amounts of new and more sophisticated anthropological research, it is perhaps surprising to find that I see no need to change the list of "fundamental insights" (pp. 72-80). I only slightly edited these basic postulates. Perhaps the most important change was to eliminate the use of the subtly sexist term "man." That modification of language use is a marker of rather large transformations in anthropology and in our popular culture.

P. J. Pelto

Contents

one

The Study of Humankind

By the beginning of the twentieth century the scholars who interested themselves in the unusual, dramatic, and puzzling aspects of man's history were known as anthropologists. They were the men who were searching for man's most remote ancestors; for Homer's Troy; for the original home of the American Indian; for the relationship between bright sunlight and skin color; for the origin of the wheel, safety pins, and pottery. They wanted to know "how modern man got that way": why some people are ruled by a king, some by old men, others by warriors, and none by women; why some peoples pass on property in the male line, others in the female line, still others equally to heirs of both sexes; why some people fall sick and die when they think they are bewitched, and others laugh at the idea. They sought for the universals in human biology and in human conduct. They proved that men of different continents and regions were physically much more alike than they were different. They discovered many parallels in human customs, some of which could be explained by historical contact. In other words, anthropology had become the science of human similarities and differences.[1]

The broadest and boldest definition of anthropology states simply that anthropology is the study of man and his works. And, in fact, only that very broad definition can include all the varied field studies, theoretical interests, and teaching areas of people who call themselves anthropolgists. Under the label *anthropology* in university catalogs, we find courses on human evolution, human genetics, linguistics, prehistory, ethnography of Middle America (and many other "culture areas"), social

1

organization, and other related topics. Anthropology is a broad umbrella that covers scholars who share an interest in the study of human life and behavior. To some extent, these interests can be categorized into four subfields: physical anthropology, archaeology, social/cultural anthropology, and linguistics.

Physical Anthropology

One important aspect of physical, or biological, anthropology is the examination of the many-sided evidence for the evolution of *Homo sapiens* from earlier forms of primate life. The comparative anatomy of contemporary primates is one type of evidence, and introductory courses in physical anthropology often begin with the comparative anatomy of humans and our nearest "cousins," the apes. The fossil evidence of human evolution from *Australopithecus* to *Homo erectus* and *Neanderthal* forms is also studied. Interest in human biological relationships with other primates also leads to a comparative study of living communities of nonhuman primates, such as gorillas, chimpanzees, and baboons.

Variations among the different populations of *Homo sapiens* are studied with the tools of modern genetics. Recent developments have led to exciting research in the inheritance of blood types, resistance to particular diseases, and the examination of biological adaptation to different physical environments. In addition, physical anthropology has become increasingly concerned with the study of human growth and constitution, relationships of nutrition and diet to growth and disease patterns, and a number of other physiological problems that bring anthropology into close contact with researchers in anatomy, radiobiology, serology, physiology, and general medicine.

Two winners of the Nobel Prize, Baruch S. Blumberg and D. Carleton Gajdusek, have made important discoveries in the complex inheritance and social transmission of certain diseases. Gajdusek uncovered a hitherto unknown slow-growing virus as the cause of a strange wasting disease among highland New Guinea peoples. Dr. Blumberg isolated the so-called "Australian antigen"—a hitherto unknown component of human blood that is associated with viral hepatitis. These examples demonstrate the ofttimes close relationships between physical anthropology and medical sciences. Many physical anthropologists, in fact, are employed in hospitals and medical schools.

Archaeology

The archaeologist studies the information about human cultures that can be gained from the careful excavation of sites of former human habitations—ancient dwellings, monuments, objects of art, tools, weapons, and other human works covered over by the soils of time. Typical course offerings in archaeology include "New World Archaeology" (concerned with the prehistoric remains of American Indian cultures), "Old World Prehistory" (including the study of stone tools, cave art, and other evidence of human activities during the great Ice Ages), "Origins of Plant Domestication," "Beginnings of Near Eastern Civilization," and various other specializations within these broad studies.

In part, archaeologists' interests in the human past resemble those of historians, and some archaeologists combine field research with a study of historical records.

Classical archaeologists, who work in the ruins of ancient civilizations of the Mediterranean and Middle East, are often found in departments of history or classics, rather than in anthropology. Archaeologists who are primarily interested in the comparative analysis of human adaptation to environment collaborate closely with other ecological scientists, especially geologists, paleobotanists, and geophysicists.

Linguistics

Linguistics is the study of language. This study is not concerned with learning to speak foreign languages fluently but rather is aimed at accurate scientific description and comparison of languages. Probably the earliest strong interest in linguistics was developed around the study of the relationships among languages, particularly when it was discovered that most of the languages of Europe were descended from a single common ancestor language—ancient Indo-European.

Recent developments in linguistics have brought linguists into increasing contact with psychologists, philosophers, and mathematicians, as they pursue such topics as psycholinguistics, metalinguistics, semantics, and communications theory.

Social/Cultural Anthropology

"Peoples and Cultures of Africa," "Ethnology of Oceania," "North American Indians," and a number of similar course titles illustrate the cultural anthropologist's concern with the infinite varieties of human behavior that have been found on the face of our globe. From this worldwide range of cultures and peoples, anthropologists search for similarities and differences that provide clues to understanding "human nature" and human cultural history.

The courses in which cultural anthropologists present their systematic comparisons and theoretical ideas are variously entitled "Comparative Economics," "Comparative Religion," "Culture Change," "Primitive Law and Government," "Social Structure," and so on. Other diverse interests of anthropologists are made clear by the names of their course listings: e.g., "Ethnomusicology," "Comparative Folklore," and "Primitive Art." Courses in which anthropological knowledge and theory are centered on the practical problems of our complex age are often titled "Applied Anthropology."

Earlier anthropologists who were mainly interested in describing the lifeway of a particular group of people were called cultural anthropologists, whereas those who studied social structure in a comparative framework called themselves social anthropologists. Now, however, these distinctions no longer apply. Most contemporary anthropologists do research that is directed to some theoretical problem that involves both social and cultural factors. Many anthropologists use the term *sociocultural* as a label to describe their work.

Cross-cultural Nature of Anthropology

Sometimes the first sign of an anthropologist-to-be is a child's fascination with Indians, lost continents, explorations in Africa, and exotic island peoples of the South Seas. The same kind of fascination with cultural differences has spurred many anthropologists to their first extensive fieldwork. When a commitment to systematic observation and comparative research is grafted onto the earlier romantic impulses, the motivations for a mature anthropological study begin to emerge.

Curiosity and fascination with the exotic is not sufficient justification for the anthropologist's interests in nonliterate, non-Western peoples, however. The more fundamental explanation is that non-Western societies provide a great range of behavioral diversity. Economic institutions, family organization, religious beliefs and practices, magic, artistic achievements, and personality types of every description provide the evidence for establishing the constants and the variants of human culture. The anthropologist feels that the fundamental principles of cultural and social systems can be discovered only through studying the whole range of human behavior patterns.

In an earlier time some anthropologists maintained that their field of study was concerned exclusively with nonliterate peoples and small-scale societies. Most anthropologists today, however, see their discipline as a general biocultural study, and recent research has diverged sharply from the previous concentration on nonliterate societies. Since the end of World War II a large part of anthropological work has been done in modern, complex societies. The research has included rural and urban communities of modern Europe, Latin America, Japan, and India, in addition to study of topics such as "the culture of a psychiatric hospital," "themes in French culture," the health food movement," "patterns of behavior in school classrooms," and "the subculture of sports groups" in the United States.

The Integration of Anthropology

> It is evident that anthropology—however specific it may often be in dealing with data—aims at being ultimately a co-ordinating science, somewhat as a legitimate holding corporation co-ordinates constituent companies. We anthropologists will never know China as intensively as a Sinologist does, or prices, credit, and banking as well as an economist, or heredity with the fullness of the genetic biologist. But we face what these more intensive scholars only glance at intermittently and tangentially, if at all: to try to understand in some measure how Chinese civilization and economics and human heredity, and some dozens of other highly developed special bodies of knowledge, do indeed interrelate in being all parts of "man"—flowing out of man, centered in him, products of him.[2]

With these words Alfred L. Kroeber expressed the idea that the stuff of anthropology is drawn from many different areas of knowledge. The research interests and types of courses taught by anthropologists reflect this great diversity. But in many situations today there are tendencies toward the fragmentation of the discipline. Physical anthropology, for example, is becoming increasingly specialized and complex in its research on the physiology, anatomy, and genetic attributes of humans. Consequently, most cultural anthropologists find themselves further and further out of touch with the newest research and information in this field. Also, the study of linguistics has become highly specialized with an intricate vocabulary of description, semimathematical modes of analysis of language structure, and extremely complex philosophical and psychological arguments over fundamental assumptions in the field.

As we view the natural history of different branches of science and philosophy, we see that diversification and separation of fields of study is a natural result of increased knowledge about the world in which we live. It is easy, therefore, to argue that gradual splitting up of the different branches of anthropology into separate disciplines would be just as natural as the differentiation of chemistry, physics, and biology from the earlier unity of general science. But most anthropologists, especially in the United States, cling stubbornly to the "holistic principle" as stated by Kroeber. Despite all tendencies toward specialization, the strong interrelatedness of human physical characteristics and behavioral systems cannot be ignored. From whatever angle the nature of the human animal is approached, we see that economic behavior, religious institutions, and other aspects of culture are deeply influenced by psychobiological characteristics. Similarly, our physical systems are affected by religion, occupation, family structure, and other social and cultural facts.

One area of study that graphically illustrates the integration of anthropology is that of health and sickness. Recent studies of sickness and health-seeking behavior have often involved research by human biologists (physical anthropologists), nutritionists, sociocultural anthropologists, and other specialists.

The disease called schistosomiasis is a good example of a problem that has been intensively studied by biocultural research teams in tropical and subtropical areas. The sickness is caused by an intestinal parasite with a complex life-cycle. Inside the human body the parasite (commonly known as the liver fluke) can remain healthy and active for years without any symptoms. For many individuals, however, later stages of infection may be very serious, resulting in liver damage, enlarged spleen, hemorrhaging, and death from heart attack.

Outside the human, the *schistosome* (liver fluke) finds an intermediate home in a particular species of water snail called *Bilomphalaria*. These snails are especially fond of the waterways and reservoirs created in irrigation projects; so the human cultural activities around intensified agriculture provide new homes for these host animals. Thus economic development projects have sometimes had the side effect of increasing the numbers of people infected by schistosomiasis as they work in the fields, wash themselves in the canals, or swim in the infected waters. The practical problems surrounding schistosomiasis involve the interaction of biological and sociocultural factors. Anthropologists have played an active role in some of the research on schistosomiasis.

The relatively new and fast growing field of medical anthropology is thus an integration of biological, cultural, social, and psychological principles.

Relationships with Other Social Sciences

Anthropologists are interested in many of the same subjects that other social scientists study. Of these, the sociologists are the most closely related, in methods and interests, to anthropology. There is indeed a good deal of both theoretical and practical overlap between anthropology and sociology. And the areas of common interest seem to have increased considerably in recent decades. Nonetheless, some general differences separate the interests and research styles of *most* anthropologists from those of *most* sociologists. These differences include:

1. Most anthropologists prefer to include study of non-Western peoples in their teaching and research; most sociologists prefer to study aspects of Western society and culture. (But growing numbers of sociologists are now immersed in studies of African, Indian, Chinese, and other societies.)
2. Most anthropologists prefer to do research on small communities, by means of observations and interviews of people in face-to-face contact. Most sociologists prefer to study larger segments of social systems, using information gathered on questionnaires or extracted from statistics on population, crime rates, employment figures, voting records, and so on. In general, sociologists feel more at home using statistical analysis than do anthropologists.
3. Anthropologists include physical anthropology as an important part of their science; sociologists concentrate their studies almost exclusively on social aspects of humankind.
4. Most anthropologists consider human cultural history to be a central concern of the discipline; the majority of sociologists leave historical studies to others, preferring modern social institutions for research topics.

The differences between anthopology and psychology are much more clearly observable; though again there are important areas of overlap. Psychologists usually study the behavior of individuals in carefully defined laboratory or experimental situations; thus, psychology is much more an experimental science than is anthropology. Psychologists are usually even less interested than sociologists in study of non-Western peoples. However, the rapidly developing field of social psychology includes cross-cultural studies and other features that are very close to the interests of psychologically oriented anthropologists. Anthropologists and psychologists also have common interests in, and much potential for, joint research on the physiology of the human brain and nervous system. A new area of cooperation has developed between psychology and anthropology in laboratory and field studies of monkeys and apes.

Anthropology also shares interests with geography. Studies of the spread of domestication of plants and animals; adaptation of peoples to particular kinds of physical environments; social and cultural characteristics of pastoral (animal-herding) societies, and a great many other areas of research are studied simultaneously by geographers and anthropologists. In regard to topics such as Islamic cultural history, Chinese culture and society, and Latin American cultural history we often find anthropologists and historians working on very similar research interests, though methods of study may be different. The full range of anthropological interests and research links the work of anthropologists with that of scholars in many other fields. This is natural and expected, for all scholars accept the principle of the interconnectedness of the universe, the unity of all life on earth, and the oneness of human history and society. Special areas of study labeled with the names of various "-ologies" are, after all, artificial segments of information chopped out of the unified web of events and things. If scholars paid careful heed to the artificial boundaries between areas of study, we might still be in the Dark Ages of human knowledge.

Summary

Since anthropology is the study of humankind, including human social, cultural, psychological, and physical characteristics, anthropological study is partly biological science, partly social science, and in part included among the humanities. In the main lines of their studies, anthropologists may be distinguished from sociologists, psychologists, physiologists, zoologists, geographers, historians, and others; but the wide-ranging interests of individual scholars make any clear boundaries among these several disciplines impossible to draw. Some of the most exciting areas of modern research are those that play havoc with the boundaries among the various disciplines. Studies of mental health and mental disorder, for example, involve the work of physiologists, psychiatrists, psychologists, sociologists, anthropologists, geneticists, biochemists, and social workers. The general areas of human evolution and cultural history similarly combine work from dozens of different branches of science and humanities.

Anthropologists have attempted to maintain a broad, holistic approach to their work. Narrow specializations generally have been avoided, as well as the splitting of anthropology into separated sub-compartments. But the strains involved in maintaining this unity of anthropology sometimes show on the faces of weary and harassed students who must spread their studies over such wide ranges of information and theory.

Notes

1. Clyde Kluckhohn, *Mirror for Man* (New York: McGraw-Hill, 1949), p. 2.
2. Alfred L. Kroeber, ed, *Anthropology Today* (Chicago: University of Chicago Press, 1953), p. xiv.

Recommended Reading

General introductory textbooks intended for freshman-sophomore courses in anthropology provide useful perspectives on the scope and content of anthropology, with illustrative materials from around the world. These introductory texts vary in their theoretical points of view, and in their selections of illustrative materials from different cultures. Here are just two of the many books now available:

Harris, Marvin. *Culture, People, Nature* (New York: Crowell, 1975).

This work is engagingly written and presents a coherent view of anthropology that emphasizes the ways in which energy, economic system, and technological factors strongly shape human cultural patterns.

Pelto, Gretel H. and Pertti J. Pelto. *The Human Adventure* (New York: Macmillan, 1976).

The Human Adventure includes more materials on contemporary social issues—e.g., the energy crisis, world population, revolutionary movements—than most anthropology texts.

two

The History of Anthropology

These are the families of the sons of Noah, after their generations, in their nations; and by these were the nations divided in the earth after the flood. *(Genesis 10:32)*

And the whole earth was of one language, and of one speech. *(Genesis 11:1)*

The biblical view of human diversity was a plausible anthropological perspective throughout the centuries before Europeans discovered the existence of the Americas, the far East, the South Seas, and the varieties of cultures south of the Sahara in Africa. To the ancient Greeks, for example, the known world and its peoples stretched from Gibraltar on the west across to India; and from some vague point south of Egypt into the equally vague northlands beyond the Danube—fabled lands inhabited by "barbarians."

Among the ancient Greeks, the historian-philosopher-anthropologist Herodotus (484—424 B.C.) was the first to travel widely in order to study at close range many different peoples and their lifeways. Like modern anthropologists he intereviewed "key informants" and recorded their statements for posterity. His writing includes the first clear statement about matrilineal, or "mother-right" descent:

They have, however, one singular custom in which they differ from every other nation in the world. They take the mother's not the father's name. Ask a Lycian who he is, and he answers by giving his own name, that of his mother, and so on in the female line.

Moreover, if a free woman marry a man who is a slave, their children are full citizens; but if a free man marry a foreign woman or lives with a concubine, even though he be the first person in the state, the children forfeit all the rights of citizenship.[1]

Although Herodotus and a few other ancient Greeks were the first people to embark on a naturalistic study of human behavior, we can turn to the Roman Tacitus for our best example of an early "ethnographic monograph" about a particular "exotic" culture. In his *Germania* (98 A.D.) Tacitus described the character, manners, and geographical setting of the German tribes. He wrote to warn fellow Romans of the strength and spirit of the Germans, for he saw them as uncorrupted barbarians who would bring about the downfall of a rapidly degenerating Rome. He noted with admiration that "no one in Germany finds vice amusing, or calls it 'up-to-date' to debauch and be debauched."[2] He also noted:

For all that, marriage in Germany is austere, and there is no feature in their morality that deserves higher praise. They are almost unique among barbarians in being satisfied with one wife each. The exceptions, which are exceedingly rare, are of men who received offers of many wives because of their rank. There is no question of sexual passion. The dowry is brought by husband to wife, not by wife to husband.[3]

After Tacitus, up to the thirteenth and fourteenth centuries, there were few scholars who attempted dispassionate observation and explanation of human behavior and society. The development of a strong religious scholarship, dating from St. Augustine, drew people toward more theological and metaphysical interpretations of human behavior. Any naturalistic, empirical investigation of human nature was discouraged by threats of harassment and persecution.

The Great Travelers: Marco Polo, Ibn Batuta, Ibn Khaldun

In the thirteenth and fourteenth centuries there were a few isolated instances of "proto-anthropological" writing. Marco Polo, having traveled in China and much of the rest of Asia for more than twenty years (1271-1295), transmitted to posterity a wealth of knowledge of peoples and customs far beyond the imaginations of his Italian contemporaries. Here is a fragment from his observations about the Tartars of Central Asia:

They have circular houses made of wood and covered with felt, which they carry with them on four-wheeled wagons wherever they go. For the framework of rods is so neatly and skillfully constructed that it is light to carry ... and I assure you that the womenfolk buy and sell and do all that is needful for their husbands and households. For the men do not bother themselves with anything but hunting and warfare and falconry. ... They have no objection to eating the flesh of horses and dogs and drinking mare's milk. ... Not for anything in the world would one of them touch another's wife; they are too well assured that such a deed is wrongful and disgraceful... .[4]

Ibn Batuta (1304-1378), the greatest Arab traveler of the Middle Ages, set off from his native North Africa on a series of travels to Russia, China, India, Sumatra, Cambodia, and then into sub-Saharan West Africa, including Timbuktu. The main lines of his twenty-eight years of travel covered something like 75,000 miles. Ibn Batuta's narrative reveals much information about relationships among the various Islamic governments of his time, as well as details of Islamic religious and cultural practices.

About the same time, another Arab scholar, Ibn Khaldun, was collecting observations and writing about the nature of human society. He was not just a collector of information and observations, like Polo and Ibn Batuta, but must be considered a profound social scientist. From his own rich experiences in various Islamic governments, and his extensive reading and observations, he attempted to organize "a study of human society in all its different forms, the nature and characteristics of each of these forms, and the laws governing its development."[5] Some of Ibn Khaldun's principles are remarkably modern, though written over 500 years ago:

1. Social phenomena obey laws, which are sufficiently constant to cause social events to follow regular, well-defined patterns and sequences.
2. These laws operate on masses and cannot be significantly influenced by isolated individuals. (He gives the example of the reformer's attempts to rejuvenate a corrupt state. These reform efforts meet with little success; the individual's efforts are submerged by overwhelming social forces.)
3. Social laws can be discovered only by gathering large numbers of facts, from which sequences and correlations can be observed.
4. Similar social laws operate in societies of the same kind of structures, however separated in time and space. (He notes similarities among nomadic Bedouins, Kurds, and Berbers.)
5. Societies are not static, for social forms change and evolve.
6. These are all social laws, not merely reflections of biological or physical factors.

The Age of Discovery

In the fifteenth century, a series of important discoveries opened the way to new knowledge of human diversity around the world. Even before the discovery of the Americas by Columbus, Portuguese, Spanish, and other seafarers had sailed around Africa and begun the exploration of unknown lands and peoples far beyond Europe's narrow borders. The fall of Constantinople (1453) brought a migration of Aristotelian scholars into western Europe, and the spread of knowledge was given impetus by the invention of the printing press (1446), and the knowledge of how to make inexpensive paper—a Chinese invention—was brought to the West by Arab traders.

The varieties of peoples and cultures around the world didn't fit well with the old, biblical versions of humankind. How could all that diversity of human groups have come about if Noah had only three sons, Shem, Ham and Japhet—"and of them the whole earth was overspread." (Genesis: 9:18-19). The Spaniards and Portuguese, busy staking out their claims to the lands and wealth of the New World, justified their cruelties to Indian peoples by declaring that the Indians were *not* descendants of Adam (through Noah's sons) and hence were outside the protective shelter of God's grace. In 1512 the pope declared to the contrary, saying that the American Indians were indeed descendants of Adam and should be treated with the same respect and human moral principles as anybody else. Despite this papal decree the Europeans continued to subjugate, exploit, and kill off the native peoples in the newly discovered areas of the world. Individual Catholic missionaries sometimes worked to protect the newly colonized peoples from excessive cruelties. In some unusual cases missionaries and explorers took the time to study the social organization and cultural patterns of the people they worked with.

The Spanish priest Fray Bernadino de Sahagun stands out as one of the greatest of the "missionary-ethnographers." During the years from 1529 to 1590 he devoted himself to collecting information about the pre-Conquest cultural life of the Aztec people of central Mexico. He had a number of bilingual Indian people working with him, writing down texts and descriptions of healing practices, everyday foods, ceremonies, the calendar, and details of social organization. Sahagun described some of his research methods as follows:

> In the said village I had all the leaders assembled, together with the lord of the village, Don Diego de Mendoza, an old man of great distinction and ability, very experienced in all civil, military, and political, and even idolatrous matters. Having met with them, I proposed what I intended to do and I asked that they give me qualified and experienced persons with whom I could talk and who would be able to answer what I asked. ... Another day the lord and the leaders came and... they pointed out to me ten or twelve leading elders and told me I could speak with them and that they would truly answer everything that might be asked of them. There were also four Latinists, to whom I had taught grammar a few years earlier. ... With these leaders and grammarians who were also leaders I conversed many days, nearly two years. ... [6]

While the conquest of new worlds and peoples in Africa, Asia, and the Americas continued in the seventeenth, eighteenth, and nineteenth centuries, hot scholarly and theological debate continued about the "descent from Adam" question. Scholars, such as the physician Paracelsus and the philosopher Giordano Bruno, maintained that Africans, South Sea Islanders, and other "physically different" people were of a different *species* from Europeans. In this instance the orthodox theological position came down on the side we now regard as "modern and progressive," for religious orthodoxy held to the view that all humanity was descended from a single ancestor. The debates between the "monogenists" (common ancestor proponents) and the "polygenists" continued into the nineteenth century, and was only intensified when Charles Darwin published his theory of biological evolution and *The Origin of Species*.

Not all scholars and writers were interested in the "single species" debates, however. Many missionaries, explorers, and other travellers were more concerned with describing those varied peoples and cultures, thus contributing to the store of natural history and ethnography about which western Europeans were eager to learn. Richard Hakluyt's *Divers Voyages Touching the Discovery of America* (1582) is perhaps the earliest collection of geographical and anthropological information that became available to scholars during the Age of Discovery. Other well-known works include the *Historia de Gentibus Septentrionalibus* (History of the People of the North) by Olaus Magnus (1555), Captain Cook's *Voyages* (1770s and 1780s), P.S. Pallas' account of his Russian journeys (1771-76), and D. Crantz' *History of Greenland*.

Jesuit priests were avid collectors and describers of ethnographic materials. They accumulated a mammoth, seventy-three-volume storehouse of information about the American Indians in the period between 1610 and 1791 (published as the *Jesuit Relations*).

The ethnographic descriptions from missionaries, travelers, and others soon played a role in the theories and arguments of the philosophers of the Enlightenment. Materials from the *Jesuit Relations* were included in John Locke's discussions of the Social Contract. Rousseau set forth his ideas about "the noble savage" based on information about the Carib Indians of Venezuela.

Gradually a field of anthropology emerged in the eighteenth and nineteenth centuries, made up of the naturalistic descriptions of peoples and their lifeways, organized and explained by theorists and philosophers. Before this fledgling field of study could advance, there were two major obstacles to overcome: (1) the predominating theological versions of human nature and human history had to be challenged along with some other western European ethnocentric biases; and (2) the methods of gathering basic ethnographic data had to be sharpened.

The conversion of ethnographic fieldwork from an amateur pastime to a scholarly profession was accomplished during the nineteenth century. The systematic techniques for collection of ethnographic data were developed in response to the realization that many of the narratives and descriptions sent back by travelers, administrators, and missionaries were romanticized, distorted, and highly superficial observations. Solid scientific study of pan-human social and cultural characteristics and the understanding of human cultural evolution would have to be based on very carefully collected information, gathered by well-trained researchers who had mastered the native languages of the people they studied.

The first "field guide" for ethnographers was actually developed before there were any professional anthropologists! The French *Société des Observateurs de l'Homme* were planning scientific expeditions to Africa and Asia; so a young philosopher, Joseph-Marie Degérando, wrote a booklet entitled *Considerations on the Various Methods to Follow in the Observation of Savage Peoples*. Although the year was 1800, some of his main ideas (if not his terminology) fit well with modern, twentieth-century anthropology. He argued, "the first means to the proper knowledge of the Savages, is to become after a fashion like one of them; and it is by learning their language that we shall become their fellow citizens." He also suggested lists of questions to ask about kinship and family structure, including "Does the father have any authority? On what principle does it appear to be based? . . . What respect have young people for the old? What are the internal bonds of society, and the foundations on which rests the unity of its members?" [7]

Degérando's excellent fieldwork instructions didn't have much effect on the explorers from the *Société des Observateurs;* the real beginnings of systematic fieldwork methods came decades later, when people who studied the varieties of cultures and languages began to occupy positions in universities. The acceptance of anthropology as a full member of the "community of scholars" came with some sweeping changes in accepted views of human history.

The Rise of Anthropology

The philosophers of the Enlightenment, using information about non-European peoples in their philosophical speculations, developed broad theories of human progress and cultural evolution that were the foundations for much of nineteenth-century social thinking. Anne Robert Jacques Turgot (1717-1781) was one of the foremost shapers of these theories, based on assumptions of a fundamental pan-human unity of capabilities:

> No doubt the mind of man everywhere contains within itself the seeds of the same achievements, but nature, not impartial in the bestowal of her gifts, has given to certain minds a fullness of talent that she has refused to others; circumstances develop these talents or leave them buried in obscurity; and from the infinite variety of such circumstances springs the inequality that marks the progress of nations.

> Barbarism makes all men equal; and in the earliest times, all those who are born with genius find almost the same obstacles and the same resources. Time passes, and societies are formed and grow: The hates of nations, and ambition—or rather avarice, the sole ambition of barbaric peoples—multiply wars and devastation. Conquests and revolutions comingle in a thousand ways, peoples, tongues, and manners. ... [8]

The speculations of Turgot and other philosophers were seriously hampered by lack of information about past times—the prehistories of European and other peoples. Theories about human cultural and biological evolution, which generally ran counter to accepted theological versions of human history, were also difficult to fit into the few thousand of years allowed for in the biblical version of the earth's origins.

Up to the beginning of the nineteenth century most scholars had accepted the age of the earth as encompassing only a few tens of thousands of years. In fact a great many serious scholars accepted the pronouncement of Archbishop Ussher, in 1650, who had calculated from careful study of the scriptures that the world was created by God exactly 4004 years before the birth of Christ. To this reckoning the theologian Lightfoot had added the demonstration that "heaven and earth, center and circumference, were created together, in the same instant, and clouds full of water...[and that] this work took place and man was created by the Trinity on the twenty-third of October, 4004 B.C. at nine o'clock in the morning." [9]

The Genesis version of the age of the earth and of humankind stood up well against philosophical speculations until archaeological and geological research began to turn up new kinds of empirical evidence—of seashells high up in the mountains, traces of past Ice Ages, and human-made stone tools buried deep in the ground.

In the 1830s and 1840s Abbe Boucher de Perthes discovered numbers of stone tools in the gravel of the river Somme, near Paris, and he began to insist on the immense antiquity of these works of human hands. Great theological and scientific argument raged, especially in France and England, over the age of these archaeological materials. Other significant archaeological finds were made both in France and England, and as early as 1825 a rhinoceros tooth had been found with a flint weapon in Kent's Cavern in England, by the Rev. J. MacEnery. The rapid accumulation of evidence about the Stone Age seriously undermined the orthodox, biblical chronology of human cultural history.

Another striking development in the accumulating evidence concerning our antiquity took place in a little river valley near Düsseldorf, Germany. There, in 1857, were found portions of a human skeleton with features very different from those of modern humans. The skull was massive, somewhat flattened on top, with extremely heavy brow ridges. The German doctor who first wrote about these human fossil remains described them as belonging to a "barbarous and savage race ... the most ancient memorial of the early inhabitants of Europe."[10] This immensely important fossil had been found in the valley of the Neander River, hence its name— Neanderthal Man.

By 1859, the year of publication of Darwin's *The Origin of Species,* leading scientists of western Europe were ready to accept the theory that earth and human-kind are very old; that the relative age of rocks, soil, and human artifacts can be read from their positions in the layers, or strata, laid down on the surface of the earth following known geological principles; and that the stone tools and skeletal remains from various sites in England, France, and elsewhere are evidence of the beginnings of human biological and cultural history dating from hundreds of thousands of years ago. Darwin's famous theory of natural selection provided a way of explaining our relations to the natural world, and for understanding the relationship of Neanderthal Man (and other such fossils) to modern *Homo sapiens.* Some scientists were quick to apply the basic principles of evolution to the nonbiological cultural materials as well.

Early Applied Anthropology

In Tasmania, where thousands were hunted down like beasts and shot, by 1835 only 203 aboriginals were left, the pitiful remnant of thousands. The last pure-blooded Tasmanian died in 1861. On the continent they did not fare much better. [Australian] Sheepherders, in order to clear the grazing-grounds more rapidly, offered them, in apparent friendliness, cakes of flour dosed with arsenic, and thus poisoned off black humanity like ground squirrels. Other ingenious native-exterminators poisoned the waterholes.[11]

The slaughter of aborigines, along with the vast inhumanity of the slave trade, aroused the consciences of many humanitarians in England and on the Continent. In 1837 the Aborigines Protection Society was founded in London, and a year later, with similar humane intentions, the Ethnological Society in Paris. The *Journal of the Ethnological Society* of London, in 1856, carried this statement:

Ethnology is now generally recognized as having the strongest claims in our attention, not merely as it tends to gratify the curiosity of those who love to look into Nature's works, but also as being of great practical importance, especially in this country, whose numerous colonies and extensive commerce bring it into contact with so many varieties of the human species differing in their physical and moral qualities both from each other and from ourselves.[12]

The study of anthropology developed, therefore, from a fusion of theoretical and practical interests. On the one hand was the scholarly curiosity concerning the Stone Age, the rise of ancient civilizations, and the "strange and exotic" customs of diverse living peoples. At the same time, many of the early anthropologists were imbued with the conviction that knowledge of human cultures would bring immediate practical advantages to people—in the reduction of human cruelty, misery, and ignorance.

The Doctrine of Cultural Evolution

Although anthropological theories of the evolution of culture were given a boost by the publication of Darwin's *The Origin of Species,* we should remember that the concepts of cultural evolution and "progress" were developed by the philosophers in the century before Darwin. They had set forth stages through which human culture supposedly had progressed, starting with the creation, the fall, and the flood, followed by organization into small groups of hunters and gatherers, then the development of pastoralism, the inventions of agriculture and the idea of private property, the growth of villages, division of labor, and thence to modern civilization.

Lewis Henry Morgan

Lewis Henry Morgan (1818-1881) is considered to be the founding father of American anthropology. Morgan was born in upstate New York, where he studied law at Union College in Schenectady, and then settled down to law practice, business, politics, and anthropological study in Rochester. As a young man, Morgan had founded the Order of the Gordian Knot at Aurora, organized around ideas of Greek mythology, secret rites, sacred paraphernalia, and other similar trappings. Somewhat later, the society was reorganized around American Indian ritual and mythology, as the Grand Order of the Iroquois. In collecting information about the Iroquois for these social activities, Morgan became interested in the Iroquois themselves and began to gather materials for more serious purposes. Soon he was deeply involved in trying to help the Iroquois fight against unscrupulous land-grabbers, while he continued his ethnographic notes. His *League of the Iroquois* (1851), the first comprehensive monograph on a North American Indian tribe, resulted from these efforts.

In working with the Iroquois, Morgan had discovered some rather "peculiar" things about the kinship terms they used to refer to their relatives. An Iroquois individual called his mother's sister by the same word that he used when referring to his mother. Also, the father's brother—indeed quite a number of other male paternal relatives—were referred to by the same word as that used for one's father. Furthermore, the whole of Iroquois society was organized into matrilineal clans (kinship groups claiming descent through females only). And when a couple married they generally settled down with the bride's kin rather than joining the husband's kin group or establishing a household of their own.

Morgan searched for an explanation of the Iroquois patterns of kinship terminology and thought he found it in the idea of "survivals." That is, if all human societies (including the Iroquois) had passed through an evolutionary stage of "group marriage"—the union of several men with several women— then the Iroquois called several people "mother" and numbers of older males "father" as a relic from that bygone stage of society.

Morgan collected information on kinship systems from many parts of the world and wove them into the fabric of an Enlightenment style theory of human progress, adding many innovations of his own. Table 1 shows the main stages of human cultural evolution from Morgan's famous book *Ancient Society.* [13]

Table 1. *Morgan's Stages of Evolution (Read from bottom up)*

Stages	Cultural Example	Differentiating Characteristics
Civilization	Europeans, Americans	Begins after the alphabet was invented
Higher Barbarism	Greeks of ancient time	Begins with use of iron
Middle Barbarism	Zuni, Hopi Indians	Begins with domestication of animals and plants
Lower Barbarism	Iroquois Indians	Begins with invention of pottery
Higher Savagery	Polynesians	Begins with use of bow and arrow
Middle Savagery	Australian aborigines	Begins with fish diet, use of fire and speech
Lower Savagery	no known examples	Before fire and speech were invented

The basic philosophical premises of Morgan's evolutionary system are similar to the ideas underlying the writings of most other well-known anthropologists of the nineteenth century. They assumed that all people are rational beings who strive to improve themselves. They assumed that humankind is part of nature, hence developing in accordance with natural laws. These laws of the universe were considered to be unchanging through time. In general, they felt that evolution proceeds from simple to complex, from unorganized to organized, and, especially, that this development is directly associated with betterment—that evolution is simultaneously progress, the march toward human perfection.

Edward B. Tylor

Edward B. Tylor was Morgan's English counterpart. In his book *Primitive Culture* (1871), he elaborated his version of the story of evolution with special concentration on religion. He believed that the earliest form of religion was "animism"—the belief that people, animals, and even trees and stones have indwelling spirits or souls. The origin of this belief and hence the origin of religion, Tylor theorized, is to be found in our seeking rationally to explain what happens in dreaming and death.

During the nineteenth century, theologians argued, following biblical interpretation, that humans had fallen from original grace and that "primitive" peoples had degenerated the furthest from the original high culture of paradise. Tylor and the evolutionists claimed, on the other hand, that peoples like the Australians were examples of the rude beginnings of all humankind and that everywhere there is progress from "savagery" toward "civilization," though some peoples (possibly due to isolation and other factors) have not progressed as far as others in this evolution.

The Development of Archaeology

During the nineteenth century, the elaboration of theories about human cultural evolution was based in considerable part on the rapid accumulation of archaeological evidence from many parts of the world. Archaeological excavations in France,

England, the Scandinavian countries, and other areas were conducted with increasing sophistication and thoroughness.

In the 1830s and 1840s, Danish archaeologists at the Copenhagen Museum developed the systematic sequence of Stone Age—Bronze Age—Iron Age, based on tools and weapons made of these materials that they dug up in Danish archaeological sites. Their work not only produced a framework for understanding the past cultural history of northern Europe (and elsewhere), but also established a basic archaeological principle—the idea of stratigraphic succession, that the sequences of layers in an archaeological site can often be used to read off the *chronological sequence* of cultural materials.

Archaeological excavations in Europe and elsewhere during the nineteenth century were a curious mixture. Some researchers were devoted scientists, dedicated to expanding human knowledge. Others were reckless looters in search of quick profit. Still others were bent on the apparently patriotic task of accumulating treasures for their respective national museums. The British excavator Layard, in search of treasures for British museums, excavated the ancient site of Nimrud in Mesopotamia with the general rule: "to obtain the largest possible number of well-preserved objects of art at the least possible outlay of time and money."[14]

The most infamous of all the looters of archaeological sites and treasures was said to be Giovanni Battista Belzoni, in the early 1800s. His own description of his first foray into archaeology must bring tears and shudders of outrage to even the most staunch-willed.

> Every step I took I crushed a mummy in some part or other. When my weight bore on the body of an Egyptian it crushed like a bandbox. I sank altogether among the broken mummies with a crash of bones, rags, and wooden cases. ... [15]

Despite the looters and the merely reckless, a great deal of sound archaeological information was amassed. In France, painstaking researchers pieced together the complex sequences of prehistoric cultures that led up to the magnificent cave art at the end of the Ice Ages. Many of the excavations in western Europe during the last part of the nineteenth century included discoveries of ancient skeletal materials, so that physical remains of our prehistoric ancestors were directly linked with the tools, weapons, and other things they manufactured. In American archaeology the nineteenth century was full of discoveries about the great pyramids, temple platforms, and other monumental remains.

Tangible support for the idea of human biological evolution also accumulated at a rapid rate in the latter part of the nineteenth century. Several fossil specimens of the Neanderthal type were found in the last half of the century, and the first clear evidence of a species of man-ape, or ape-man, was discovered in the 1890s by Eugene Dubois in southeast Asia. His famous discovery of "Java Man" (*Pithecanthropus erectus*) was a striking confirmation of Darwin's theories of evolution as applied to *Homo sapiens.* The Java specimen—consisting of the top of the skull plus some long bones—appeared to be "halfway between" apelike and humanlike features.

Thus, by the end of the nineteenth century there was an impressive mass of information attesting to human biological evolution—physical changes in our ancient ancestors that must have required at least several hundreds of thousand of years. At the same time, the archaeological evidence showed that human cultural development had taken different forms and sequences in different geographical locations. Yet everywhere there was evidence for a Stone Age of humankind that must have gone on during the hundreds of thousands of years that it took for human biological evolution.

The Reaction to Cultural Evolutionism

The family portrait of our past cultural evolution, as put together by Morgan, Tylor, and many other theorists, seemed a simple and straightforward progression. Everywhere and among all peoples it seemed that the same general stages had occurred—from stone to bronze to iron; from animism to polytheism to monotheism; from hunting-and-gathering to simple cultivation to plow agriculture; and similar progressions in other aspects of culture and social organization. Many western European scholars believed that the same sequences of development were predestined in human history *and* that they represented *progress* and improvement in human mind and body. Thus they believed that monotheism (especially Christian monotheism) was superior to other religions, that the monogamous nuclear family was inherently more moral and excellent than any other form of family arrangement, and that most other features of western European culture similarly represented the finest developments of the human intellect.

There was a good deal of underlying racism and colonialism affecting these theoretical positions. For the more blatantly imperialistic thinkers these ideas of a straight line of cultural evolution—ever higher and higher—were sufficient excuse for the many ways in which Europeans exploited and dominated non-European peoples.

But the cultural evolutionists' theoretical ideas were not simple concoctions in service of colonialism and economic imperialism. For many anthropologists and other scholars, including Tylor and Morgan, the ideas were intended as *humanitarian* principles that countered conservative theological ideas of a "fall from grace," and asserted that all human groups *should be helped* to attain the higher levels of "cultural development." Moreover, many cultural evolutionists believed that, *in principle,* all human groups were equally capable of "civilization."

As the nineteenth century neared its close, some anthropologists began to have serious doubts about the Morgan and Tylor theories of cultural evolution. These anti-evolutionist scholars doubted that all human societies pass through the same stages of development. They also doubted that the past thousands of years had been a chronicle of upward progress. They advanced the idea that human cultural history is best understood as the result of the diffusion of cultural elements and ideas in various geographical areas, with some areas left out, or "marginal" to the brisk flow of cultural contacts.

In retrospect one can say that the reaction against doctrines of cultural evolutionism represented the first in a series of shock waves in the intellectual community. The reaction to the power and persuasiveness of western European culture, at the turn of the century, was a pale harbinger of the doubts and critique that shook Western social thought in the years following World War I.

In England the most extreme anti-evolutionists were W.J. Perry and Sir Grafton Elliot Smith, who claimed that peoples of the world were so unimaginative that practically all cultural developments must have been invented only once, among one gifted people—the Egyptians— from which the new ideas and cultural features diffused to various places around the world. The metallurgy, agriculture, architecture, complex social system, religious practices, and other cultural attainments of the Mayan, Aztec, and Incan civilizations of the Americas, for example, must have been "borrowed" from the center of all things—Egypt.

Austrian anthropologists also developed an anti-evolutionist school of thought in the early twentieth century, in part reflecting a partial return to religious ideas. A number of theologically trained scholars, the most notable of whom was Pater Wilhelm Schmidt, developed and expanded the "Vienna school" of diffusionism. One of the central tenets of this group was that the most marginal people on the earth still maintained a belief in "one high god"—a belief away from which much of the rest of the world had been corrupted. Schmidt and other leaders of the Vienna school believed that original human culture developed somewhere in Asia, and from the *Urkultur* there developed several distinct *Kulturkreise* ("culture complexes") in different environments. Great migrations of peoples carried these ancient *Kulturkreise* into widely separated parts of the globe. For example, *the matrilineal Kulturkreis,* with its hoe cultivation, plank boats, moon mythology, rectangular houses with gabled roofs, and men's secret societies was supposedly carried to both the New Guinea area and to Africa. The *Kulturkreise* anthropologists have been criticized heavily for weaknesses of theory, but they frequently are applauded for their extensive fieldwork.

In American anthropology, one single individual stands out as the man who "overthrew" cultural evolutionist theories. The man was Franz Boas. Boas was educated in Germany, taking his degree in geography and physics. His professors had guided him to a firm empiricism, insisting that facts come first and theory later. During geographical fieldwork in Baffinland (1883-84), he realized that his main interests tended toward the study of people instead of climate and physical landscape; so he became an anthropologist, ultimately taking a joint position at Columbia University and the American Museum of Natural History (1895). Columbia University quickly became a focal point of anthropological activity, as growing numbers of Boasian students began extensive field studies among American Indians. Clark Wissler, Alfred Kroeber, Robert Lowie, Margaret Mead, Ruth Benedict, and Melville Herskovits are among the better known of Boas' students.

It is hard for us now to realize that in the 1890s there were still bands of Indians, threatened but not yet crushed by the waves of homesteaders, gold miners, railroad workers, army troops, and other settlers of the American West. To Boas and his students, every day spent in one's library theorizing about evolution, cultural history, and other vague, abstract ideas, meant one day's loss of priceless, irretrievable ethnographic data. So they went out in the summers and at every other opportunity, with small amounts of expensive money provided by the museum, to collect information and cultural artifacts from the Dakota, Cheyenne, Blackfoot, Crow, Apache, and others. Boas himself carried out extensive fieldwork among the Kwakiutl and other tribes of the British Columbia seacoast.

From the accumulating masses of ethnographic data on American Indians, Boas and his followers shaped a strongly anti-evolutionary theory. They denounced Morgan's stages as figments of imagination, unsupported by evidence. The complexities of ethnographic information do not fit into neat stages, they claimed. For example, several Indian tribes of the Great Plains had given up settled agricultural life in favor of nomadic buffalo hunting—the reverse of the Morgan-Tylor evolutionary sequences. They saw the history of humankind as a "tree of culture," branching, intertwining, and budding off. Each branch represented a unique cultural complex, to be understood in terms of its own unique history rather than compared to cultural complexes in other world regions in some grand scheme of "stages of evolution." Some of the differences between this "culture historical" and the evolutionary perspective on human culture can be seen in figure 1.

The new "American school" of anthropology also:

1. Denied the idea that development could be equated with progress or better-ment.
2. Refused to consider widely separated cultures as representative of broad "culture types," such as the all-embracing category "savagery."
3. Organized the world of ethnographic data into "culture areas," each thought to be unique in culture history, with a resulting distinctive array of culture elements, or traits.

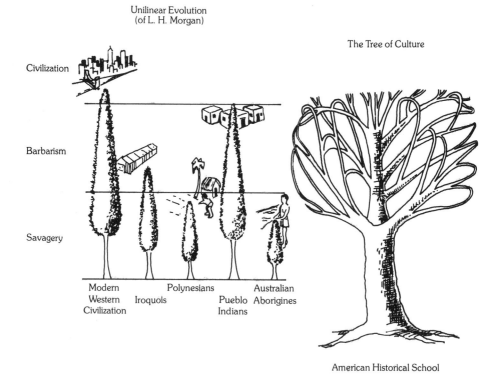

Figure 1. *Two views of cultural history.*

The differences between evolutionists and anti-evolutionist views often have obscured certain fundamental agreements. Both emphasized the rationality and humanity of primitive peoples. They were in agreement that cultural differences are due to cultural history and not biological inequalities. And both schools of thought were fundamentally opposed to the theological view that simpler peoples have "degenerated" from a state of original paradise. Evolutionists and anti-evolutionists alike constructed their theories by interrelating evidence from human biology, archaeology, study of languages, and ethnography.

Psychological and Configurational Studies

It is always the individual that really thinks and acts and dreams and revolts.[16]

This credo was written by Edward Sapir, one of Boas' most brilliant students, in reaction to what he felt to be the depersonalization inherent in the study of culture complexes, diffusion of customs, and reconstruction of cultural history. Human beings had come to be looked on as passive "culture carriers" without individual significance. In a series of papers and seminars, Sapir and a few other American anthropologists began in the 1920s and '30s to work toward an inclusion of psychological study in anthropology. One of Sapir's articles was entitled "Why Cultural Anthropology Needs the Psychiatrist."

Another of Boas' students, Margaret Mead, became interested in psychiatry and the relationships of personality and culture. For her first major fieldwork she set out to study psychological problems of adolescent Samoans. *Coming of Age in Samoa* (1928) was a pioneer effort in this new anthropological direction.

In a series of seminars during the 1930s at Columbia University, Ralph Linton (anthropologist) and Abram Kardiner (psychiatrist) collaborated in producing a new approach to psychologically oriented anthropology. Kardiner and Linton formulated the idea of "basic personality." The "basic personality" of a given people is thought of as that pattern of psychological characteristics common to all or most of the members of the society brought about by similarities in child-training practices. According to this perspective, the basic personality of a society is reflected in many areas of custom—particularly in religious beliefs and practices, art, mythology, and popular fantasies.

Cora DuBois applied this general frame of theory in *The People of Alor* (1944). Among the Alorese, located on one of the easternmost islands of Indonesia, DuBois gathered information about child training and individual dreams, biographies of individuals, as well as data about economic, social, and ritual-cultural patterns. She also obtained responses to Rorschach (ink-blot) tests and other psychological materials. Her findings suggested that Alorese children suffered great anxieties about their feeding and care, leading to food anxieties and other personality characteristics among the adults. These elements of personality in turn explained themes about food, hunger, and other anxieties in religious rituals, folktales, and individual dreams.

Culture-and-personality studies developed rapidly in the 1940s, and many anthropologists began to use personality tests in the course of fieldwork among the American Indians, peoples of the South Sea Islands, and other parts of the world. Interest also developed concerning mental illness and types of "abnormality" in non-literate societies. All these studies expressed a strong, continuing interrelationship between anthropological and psychological theories of human behavior.

Another reaction to the piecemeal cataloging of customs and complexes developed into what have been called "configurational studies." Ruth Benedict's

Patterns of Culture (1934) is the best known expression of this trend. Using the Pueblo Indians of the Southwest, the Kwakiutl of British Columbia, and the Dobu of the South Pacific for her main examples, she attempted to demonstrate that each culture is not just a random collection of customs haphazardly "borrowed" or diffused from surrounding cultures. Each culture, she maintained, is organized around some central configuration of ideas. Among the Pueblos it is an "Apollonian" moderation and restraint in all things. Kwakiutl culture, on the other hand, is supposedly pervaded by individualistic, megalomaniacal competition for prestige and honor. And Dobuan culture is characterized by a paranoid, sorcery-ridden hostility of all against all. In each case, the economy, kinship patterns, religious practices, and other major elements of custom are all thought to be shaped and interrelated by one dominant motif.

Many anthropologists felt that Benedict's configurations were too simple and could only be maintained by ignoring much contrary evidence. M.E. Opler advanced the idea of "themes" of culture. Using Apache culture as an example, he suggested that a system of several themes, rather than a single configuration, better expressed the organization of a given culture. Other anthropologists have developed the study of cultural values and postulates in similar attempts to describe the thematic inter-relatedness of human cultural systems.

Functionalist Anthropology

In the 1950s the main lines of anthropology in both America and Europe were influenced strongly by the so-called structural-functional school of social theory. Several writers of the nineteenth century, including Herbert Spencer, Fustel de Coulanges, and Auguste Comte, developed theories of human social behavior that placed special emphasis on the ways that social institutions and cultural complexes functioned to maintain the fundamental social system. Some of these lines of social thought likened societies or communities to biological organisms, in which social institutions, such as "religion" and clans, played roles analogous to the organs in a physiological system.

The French scholar Emile Durkheim set forth a theory of the origins and functions of religion. He amassed evidence to show that in Australian totemic practices each social group, clan, or other kin group worships a particular totemic animal, or other natural phenomenon, and in so doing such groups are really worshipping themselves. The totemic animal or plant seems to be a symbol of the social group itself. Durkheim concluded:

> In a general way, it is unquestionable that a society has all that is necessary to arouse the sensation of the divine in minds, merely by the power that it has over them; for to its members it is what a god is to his worshippers... religious force is nothing other than the collective and anonymous force of the clan. ... [17]

His studies of other human institutions and customs also dwelled heavily on the way they contribute to the maintenance of society.

Durkheim's writings strongly influenced A.R. Radcliffe-Brown, a British anthropologist who had done fieldwork among the Andaman Islanders off the east coast of India. Radcliffe-Brown became a leading figure in British social anthropology during the period before and after World War II. He shared the limelight of functional studies with another famous anthropologist, Polish-born Bronislaw Malinowski.

Malinowski had done his doctoral work in mathematics and had also studied physics and chemistry. While on a rest from his studies, he read Frazer's *Golden Bough* (1890) and was inspired to study anthropology. After a period of study in London, he went to the Trobriand Islands, off the coast of New Guinea, and spent the entire duration of World War I engaged in research on the language, social organization, religious economic practices, and nearly every other aspect of the Trobriand way of life. Very few field-workers have so thoroughly immersed themselves in the daily lives of a people for purposes of anthropological study.

The Trobriand Islanders, like the Lycians described by Herodotus, are matrilineal in kinship organization, and Malinowski realized that they constituted a crucial test of Freud's Oedipus complex theory. According to Freud's view, all peoples everywhere are supposed to experience the Oedipal problem: the management of aggression toward one's father because of sexual jealousies concerning one's mother, accompanied by suppressed sexual longing for the mother. Among the matrilineal Trobrianders, however, Malinowski found that a growing boy's hostilities were directed to his maternal uncle because that uncle was the person who had authority over the boy and trained him for adult life. A Trobriand boy's father was a friendly, helpful person and exercised little or no authority over his son. Malinowski also found that sexual guilt over forbidden desires involved not the mother, but the sister. Thus the ethnographic data from the matrilineal Trobrianders suggested sharp revisions in Freudian psychological theory.

As Malinowski wrote and published more of his materials, a new theoretical framework took shape. To him, cultural practices formed a tightly interrelated network, the whole of which was to be understood in terms of relationships to the psychobiological needs of individuals in society. While Durkheim and Radcliffe-Brown interpreted magic and religion as serving the needs of *societies* as organisms, Malinowski pointed to the way in which these practices and beliefs could be understood as responses to the needs of the *individual* human organism.

For example, Malinowski noted that the Trobriand Islanders (and their neighbors) did not use magic in safe seagoing operations near shore. For such ventures their canoe-building and sailing techniques were perfectly adequate. But when they had to sail farther out, where sudden storms or other unforeseen events could overtake the sailors and render useless all knowledge, skills, and techniques, the individuals experienced helpless anxiety. Magical acts, Malinowski felt, served to relieve such anxiety.

The "functionalist school" of anthropology thus developed two differing theoretical tendencies. Malinowskian functional interpretation often emphasized the needs of individuals. Followers of Durkheim and Radcliffe-Brown stressed the needs and requirements of a social system. Both types of functionalism developed a strong bias against historical studies, for they attempted analysis of a sociocultural system operating at a given time period. Functionalist theory led to great improvements in field research. Analysis of the functional importance of particular customs and institutions requires more thorough and systematic gathering of information than does simple cataloguing of customs.

As newer trends in anthopological theory have come to the fore it has become fashionable to declare that "functionalism is dead." On the other hand, some scholars have claimed that "everyone is a functionalist." The fact is that the great majority of anthropological theorists have incorporated major portions of structuralist-functionalist ideas, particularly concerning the ways that social institutions are highly interrelated and serve to maintain aspects of societal integration. When Marxist scholars claim, for instance, that the teaching in a school curriculum "supports the capitalistic system," they are asserting a functionalist observation.

Ecological Anthropology and Neo-Evolutionism

A thread of environmentalism had always been present in anthropology, but a truly ecological perspective did not gain much attention until the 1960s. One of the early proponents of "cultural ecology" was Julian Steward, who, during the 1930s, studied the close interrelationships between resources (especially food) and the modes of social organization among Indians of Nevada and eastern California. Steward felt that in each social group there is a "cultural core" of activities and beliefs whereby they make their living and maintain their political integrity. The core cultural patterns are closely interrelated with environmental resources, though it is too strong to say that the environment *determines* the cultural core. Technology is an important component in ecological analysis, for groups with different technological capabilities and energy sources are likely to have very different social organization and economic patterns, even when they live in approximately the same environmental situations.

Middle-class people are once again becoming more aware of the environment and its demands with the growing energy shortage. Poor people in the inner cities have long been aware of environmental features—during long, cold winters and hot summers. In Chicago, some people live close to the lakeshore beaches; others make do with the city's fire hydrants—even at the risk that firefighters might not be able to put out the fire.

Julian Steward and other ecological anthropologists reintroduced a modified cultural evolutionism into anthropological theory. The old "stages of evolution" were no longer useful; assumptions about "progress" and western European superiority were discarded. Instead the ecological perspective suggested that broadly similar cultural developments would occur wherever geographical features and environmental resources were similar. For example, the rise of civilizations in the Middle East and in central Mexico had followed similar patterns. With increased food production and population concentration there developed a number of small "king-doms" with increasingly stratified social systems. Cycles of warfare followed as these small states broadened their competition for scarce resources. Gradually, in both Mesopotamia and in Mexico, empires came into being as the strong city-states conquered and incorporated their neighbors.

Effective research in ecological anthropology requires intensive study of plant and animal resources, agricultural techniques, energy flow, and the integration of these core features with other social and cultural patterns. Rappoport's *Pigs for the Ancestors* (1968), an excellent illustration of this approach, focused on New Guinea. He was able to demonstrate that the ceremonial cycle of pig feasts, political alliances, and patterns of warfare are all closely integrated with the carrying capacity of the lands (for pig raising). When the number of pigs approaches the carrying capacity, a new cycle of pig slaughter is initiated, along with new rounds of warfare.

The sacred cattle of India provide a vivid demonstration of the ways in which the ecological approach has led to the reexamination of some old anthropological cliches. The presence of millions of cattle roaming the fields and byways of India, untouchable because of religious taboos against eating them, had been a favorite example of the powers of religious beliefs over practical economics. According to the earlier view those cattle were "just wasted." Marvin Harris[18] and other researchers have now demonstrated that, quite to the contrary, the cattle are essential to the highly adapted low-energy farming system of India. The cattle produce the bullocks that pull the carts and plows, and they also produce the dung that is burned for fuel in people's homes. In ecological terms it would be very wasteful to eat them.

The ecological and evolutionist theory of Steward, Rappaport, Harris, and many others represents a strong materialistic trend in anthropology, countering the essentially idealistic and "mentalistic" theoretical focus of the first half of the twentieth century. This materialism runs parallel to new lines of Marxist anthropology that is primarily a product of the 1970s. However, most ecologically oriented anthropologists are not Marxists; conversely, some Marxist anthropologists regard ecological ideas as conservative and "bourgeois."

The anthropology of Claud Levi-Strauss is a special chapter in recent social thought that defies easy categorization. Levi-Straussian "structuralism" is aimed at the study of myths, language, social organization, and other human cultural products, in an attempt to delineate pan-human similarities in deep-lying mental processes. The analysis involves the search for ordered relationships in symbols, metaphors, and grammatical forms. Those concerns would appear to be solidly "mentalistic," but Levi-Strauss and his followers claim that their study is solidly materialistic, and that they have close affinities with Marxism. At times Levi-Strauss also uses ecological interpretation.

The difficulties in placing Levi-Straussian anthropology in perspective lie partially in the fact that much of his argument is nonempirical—philosophical discussion rather than hypothesis testing through field research. Structuralism, together with some Marxist anthropology, is part of a humanistic thread that has always been part of the complex fabric of anthropology. To some writers the materials from ethnographies and other products of non-European peoples are a special kind of literary philosophy, to be understood and appreciated in the same way that we respond to Joyce's *Ulysses* or Castenada's *The Teachings of Don Juan.*

The Practical Side of Anthropology

Throughout the rise of anthropology there has always been a strong applied aspect to the studies. As mentioned earlier, many of the nineteenth-century anthropologists were motivated by intentions similar to those of the Aborigines Protection Society, to protect non-European peoples from the harmful encroachments of industrial "civilization." On the other hand, many anthropologists, especially in the British, French, Dutch, and other colonies, were hired by colonial administrations to aid in the governing of native peoples.

After World War I, Franz Boas, in many respects the spiritual leader of anthropology, devoted much energy to campaigning against racism, nationalism, and war. In fact, anthropologists were the first social scientists to advocate actively for the intellectual equality of all peoples. Consequently, anthropologists have challenged the misuse of intelligence tests in comparing different cultural groups. During the 1930s and early 1940s a number of anthropologists worked with the Bureau of Indian Affairs and the U.S. Department of Agriculture in the attempts to bring "New Deal" reforms to Indian groups.

In addition to defending the lands and economic assets of Indian groups, anthropologists have also defended the religious and cultural practices of non-European peoples. The ethnologist James Mooney of the Bureau of Indian Affairs was disciplined (in 1918) for his participation in Indians' efforts to gain legally incorporated status for their peyote religion. Later, in 1937, a national attempt to outlaw the peyote religion was counteracted by the efforts of a group that included Boas, Kroeber, and Hrdlička—three of the most prominent figures in American anthropology.

During World War II anthropologists were called upon to make their special knowledge helpful to the U.S. and Allied cause. Ethnologists reshaped ethnographic materials into manuals and handbooks about New Guinea, peoples of southeast Asia, survival manuals for deserts and jungles, and "how to win the support and friendship of native peoples." Other anthropologists studied the cultural characteristics of major nations—both enemies and allies—to provide information for military decisions as well as for handbooks on "how to understand the British." Ruth Benedict's *Chrysanthemum and the Sword* (1946) concerning Japanese national culture and character, is one of the best known of those wartime products.

Twenty years later, during the Vietnam War, some anthropological research was focused on the peoples and cultures of the war zone, but this time such "practical anthropology" on behalf of the war effort was far from popular. In fact the American Anthropological Association launched an investigation to see if anthropologists had been involved in unethical practices in connection with CIA work in Thailand, Burma, and Vietnam. Most anthropologists have taken the position that their first ethical concern is for the peoples and communities they study, and all effort must be taken to protect their anonymity and security .

Since the 1960s a large number of anthropologists have been involved in community mental health programs, public health projects, innovative projects of educational reform, nutrition programs, and a large number of other applied areas. A growing number of anthropologists have been hired directly by Indian community organizations for research and applied work in connection with land claims, development of local resources, and revitalization of culturally distinct ceremonial patterns. In recent years there have been instances in which anthropological texts and advisors have been used to re-create and rejuvenate ceremonial dances and paraphernalia in groups seeking to assert their ethnic cultural identity.

Anthropologists' focus on community-based field research makes them especially likely to become involved in applied problems, even when their original intent may have been "pure" research. As Schensul and Schensul have described,

> This involvement in community life is increased by living in the community, developing a personal and reciprocal network of friends and blending in unobstrusively in community activities. ... Anthropologists begin to share the world view of the residents and identify with their values and perspectives; ... see on a firsthand basis the community's relationship to the wider political system and the inequities that exist in that relationship; ... [and] get a close-up view of community needs and problems.[19]

Trends in the Seventies and Eighties

Some of the distinct tendencies in contemporary anthropology include:

1. Continued growth of the ecological-evolutionist theoretical perspective, including growing interest in the ecological, environmental problems of modern society. (The central importance of energy in shaping social organization was being advocated by anthropologist Leslie White during the 1930s, but no one paid much attention to him.)
2. The decline in new positions and opportunities for anthropologists in the universities will push more people into applied positions, in the federal government, health and mental health facilities, agricultural programs, and private industry.
3. The trend toward study of complex modern sociocultural systems has had a steady growth since the mid-sixties and will undoubtedly continue.
4. The ecological-evolutionist frame of reference is fostering a growth in integrated biocultural research. In areas such as medical anthropology and population studies, there are signs of increased integration of biological and cultural anthropology, with strong participation from archaeology as well.
5. The center of gravity of anthropology has definitely shifted from studies outside the United States to a predominance of research closer to the home bases of anthropologists. A great deal of research is now being carried out in urban communities, schools, health facilities, and other sectors of modern society.

6. Methodological sophistication, including use of complex statistics, computerized simulations, and other quantitative research, has grown rapidly since the mid-sixties and will continue to develop, though a balance is being struck in favor of mixing quantitative and qualitative (ethnographic) research methods. This will be examined further in chapter 3.

7. Anthropology, like all academic disciplines, is sensitive to the currents of social thought in the wider world. The trends that arose in the aftermath of the Vietnam War have strongly affected anthropological thought. Marxist radical anthropology will continue to play a role in anthropological circles, especially among the growing numbers of Third World anthropologists. Also, the women's, or feminist, movement has had strong impact on anthropology, perhaps more so than in most other disciplines. Many anthropologists were surprised to realize how strongly the discipline had been biased toward males and male-oriented analysis of cultural history, despite the strong influence of Margaret Mead, Ruth Benedict, and others. Most anthropologists have stopped using "man and his culture," and a number of textbooks have changed their titles and their language in order to eliminate the sexism inherent in earlier forms of language use.

Notes

1. G. Rawlinson, trans., *The History of Herodotus* (New York: Dutton, 1945) , p. 89.

2. H. Mattingly, trans., *Tacitus on Britain and Germany* (London: Penguin, 1948), p. 117.

3. Ibid., p. 115.

4. R.E. Latham, trans., *The Travels of Marco Polo* (London: Penguin, 1958), p. 67.

5. Charles Issawi, trans. and arr., *An Arab Philosophy of History* (London: John Murray, 1950), pp. 7—9.

6. A. López Austin, "Sahagun's Work and the Medicine of the Ancient Nahaus" in *Sixteenth Century Mexico: The Work of Sahagun,* ed. M.S. Edmonson (Albuquerque: University of New Mexico Press, 1974), pp. 115—116.

7. J.M. Degérando, *The Observation of Savage Peoples,* trans. and ed. F.C.T. Moore (Berkeley: University of California Press, 1969), pp. 88—89.

8. Works of A.R.J. Turgot (1727—81) quoted in J.S. Slotkin, *Readings in Early Anthropology* (Chicago: Aldine, 1965) pp. 360—62.

9. Homer W. Smith, *Man and His Gods* (Boston: Little, Brown and Co., 1953), p. 324.

10. T.K. Penniman, *A Hundred Years of Anthropology,* 2d rev. ed., (London: Gerald Duckworth and Co., Ltd., 1952), p. 68.

11. H.R. Hays, *From Ape to Angel* (New York: Alfred A. Knopf, 1958), p. 85

12. Ibid., pp. 294—97.

13. Lewis H. Morgan, *Ancient Society* (New York: Holt, Rinehart and Winston, 1877).

14. Frank Hole and Robert F. Heizer, *An Introduction to Prehistoric Archaeology,* 3rd ed (New York: Holt, Rinehart and Winston, 1973), pp. 45-50.

15. Ibid., pp. 47—48.

16. Edward Sapir, "Do We Need a Superorganic?" *American Anthropologist* (1917): 441—47.

17. Émile Durkheim, *The Elementary Forms of the Religious Life,* trans. Joseph Ward Swain (New York: Collier Books, 1961), pp. 236 ff.

18. Marvin Harris, *Cows, Pigs, Wars, and Witches* (New York: Random House, 1974)

19. Stephen L. Schensul and Jean J. Schensul, "Advocacy and Applied Anthropology" in *Social Scientists as Advocates* ed. George H. Weber and George J. McCall (Beverly Hills: Sage, 1978), p. 154.

three

Methods of Anthropological Research

The field of anthropology may be looked on as a "subculture," with its own social organization, customs, values, and ways of doing things. In this chapter we shall examine briefly the "customs" and procedures that anthropologists employ in the search for information about the nature of the human animal.

Fieldwork is undoubtedly the favorite activity of anthropologists. Until recently the research in all the subfields of anthropology was frequently pursued in out-of-the-way places—in Africa, the Arctic, or the South Pacific. An anthropologist's first field trip—particularly if it deals with an isolated society, far from cities and "civilization"—is regarded as an initiation rite after which he or she is "never the same again." Those few anthropologists who have concentrated on library research and avoided the risks and rigors of fieldwork are sometimes looked down on by the rest of the profession.

The romantic aura around fieldwork often obscures the fact that the anthropologist collects information in the field for later painstaking work at home—in the laboratory and the library. For every month spent in Africa, the jungles of New Guinea, rural Latin America, or in an inner-city community, the anthropologist must spend many months analyzing and writing up the findings.

Archaeology

Nearly everyone who has watched adventure shows on television or has read one of the many accounts of finding lost cities or ancient treasures has some mental images about archaeological research. The idea of digging recurs over and over in our stereotype of the archaeologist, and the field project of an archaeologist is often referred to as a "dig."

What is not generally known, however, is the highly developed inventory of techniques the archaeologist employs in accomplishing his or her fieldwork objectives.

1. Meticulous care is taken that excavated materials are not damaged in the process of digging.
2. The position and context of every object excavated is recorded by a combination of drawings, notes, and photographs so that the archaeologist can later establish with great accuracy which items found in an excavation belong together in a particular complex of materials for a particular time period.
3. All significant associated items are collected and recorded: soil samples, remains of animal and vegetable material, types of rocks and other geological specimens, and all kinds of other materials associated with the monuments, buildings, burial goods, jewels, artwork, stone tools, weapons, or other human handiwork that the archaeologist uncovers.
4. Complex equipment, ranging from infrared cameras and high powered microscopes to electronic computers, are among the tools that may be needed in this research.

Well-financed amateur archaeologists who report amazing finds of "lost cities," "fantastic works of art," and "untranslated inscriptions" are often found to be despoilers of archaeological materials because they do *not* attend carefully to the major requirements of mapping and recording mentioned above. When an archaeological find is dug up carelessly, there is usually no way to establish the time sequences of materials, the relationships of various objects to one another, and other information crucial to scientific study.

In order to preserve data and materials, the archaeologist often must often bring a portable laboratory to the fieldwork location. Having set up the equipment at an archaeological site (often the selection of the site itself is the result of months of painstaking exploration and surveying), the archaeologist maps the main outlines within which he or she will work. The places to be excavated are divided into carefully measured tracts, and each excavator goes to work in a particular tract, exercising great care not to damage any materials as they are dug up. When the archaeologist finds any significant object—a tool, a skeleton, a scrap of a work of art—it must be uncovered very slowly, sometimes using such fine tools as dental picks, toothbrushes, and small paint brushes in order to avoid damage.

One of the tragedies of earlier archaeology is the vast numbers of materials that were destroyed in the process of excavation. Concerning the nineteenth-century British archaeologist Layard and his excavations at Nimrud in Mesopotamia, Hole and Heizer commented, "though he sorely regretted it ... Layard saw many of the treasures disintegrate before his eyes. Frescoes, sculpture, and metal work frequently crumbled to bits when exposed to air and handling. Layard, in common with his competitors, had no knowledge of how to preserve the priceless objects and no time in which to experiment on techniques of conservation."[1]

Artist's reconstruction of prehistoric big-game hunt, based on archaeological evidence in central Mexico.

Of course, scientific archaeologists are not concerned only with the preservation of art objects and other spectacular materials. Their techniques are intended above all for preserving as much as possible of the *information* still remaining from past human activities in an area. Often seemingly humble remains such as *coprolites* (dessicated or fossilized remains of ancient human feces) are more valuable in informational terms (e.g., about diet and intestinal parasites) than are fancy pottery wares or other works of art.

When the archaeologist has the thousands and thousands of items excavated, marked, recorded, classified, and shipped safely back to the home laboratory, the fieldwork stage of research is over and the hard work of scientific analysis begins in earnest.

Although our discussion has focused here on "the archaeologist," it is well to keep in mind that archaeology is a teamwork activity. Seldom is an archaeological excavation carried out entirely by a single person. The usual field team will include at least a half dozen workers, and in any full-blown archaeological work there are likely to be specialists from other disciplines and subdisciplines, working on geological materials, analysis of mineral deposits, pollen, identification of bones, and a great many other specialized activities.

Dating Archaeological Remains

A major methodological problem that faces the archaeologist is the matter of chronology—establishing time periods and sequences for materials that have no written evidence of dates attached to them. Archaeological publications are full of time charts of cultural materials—put together from pieces of information gleaned from hundreds of different excavations. Some of the major methods of establishing sequences and dates for archaeological materials are described below.

Stratigraphic Evidence.   If an archaeological site is relatively undisturbed, it often can be assumed that materials found close to the surface are newer or younger than materials found deep in the ground.

Association with Plant and Animal Remains.   For example, flint handaxes found with the bones of long-extinct types of elephants, mammoths, and other animals are among the important chronological clues for early humans in western Europe. Similarly, the bones of extinct forms of camels, horses, and bison found with Indian artifacts help to establish relative ages of some North American archaeological remains.

Pollen Analysis.   Pollen grains found in association with archaeological finds may indicate what kinds of plants grew in the area at the time the materials were left on the ground. Particular combinations of plants may have been characteristic of the area at only certain time periods in the past.

Dendrochronology   (tree-ring dating). Tree-rings display variable patterns of spacing, depending on the wetness or dryness of particular years. Each sequence of years forms a unique pattern of rings. Many of the rich archaeological remains in Arizona and New Mexico have been dated by systematic tree-ring analysis of the timbers found in the sites.

Calendar Dating.   Some advanced civilizations, such as those of the Maya in Middle America and the Egyptians and Sumerians in the Old World, had calendrical systems, and dates of some archaeological materials may be interpolated from carved inscriptions. The big problem is the deciphering and analyzing of the calendrical systems.

Cross-dating from Other Cultural Materials.   Sometimes archaeological sites in Europe have coins included in them for which nearly exact dates are obtainable. This establishes that the site *cannot be older* than those dated coins, though it may be younger. Whereas the presence of coins may be unusual, a more frequent occurrence is the presence of pottery materials from other well-studied locations.

Association with Extinct Shorelines and Other Geological Features.   In northern Europe, where the land continues to rise out of the sea at a relatively constant rate, archaeological finds that were originally at the seashore, or at the edge of a lake, can be dated by calculation of the approximate time it has taken for that shoreline to rise so far from the water. A striking case of this sort is a series of rock carvings on a cliff in northern Norway which could only have been reached by boat. Since the carvings are now a number of feet above sea level, it is estimated that the works of art are several thousands of years old.

Radiological Dating.   Dating by the potassium-argon and radiocarbon methods represent some of the major breakthroughs in archaeological technology of recent decades. The radiocarbon method was developed shortly after World War II and is now an essential step in many archaeological studies. The method is based on the fact that plants and animals contain fixed amounts of a radioactive isotope of carbon, called C^{14}, which deteriorates at a constant rate after the death of the organism, leaving ordinary carbon (C^{12}).

The C^{14} is dissipated from the previously organic material at the rate of approximately *one half* every 5700 years. By electronically measuring the amount of radioactive carbon still remaining in a sample (piece of wood, charcoal, bark, plant fibers, antler, etc.) archaeologists can estimate the approximate antiquity of the materials. Most of the measurable radioactive carbon is gone from a sample after about 45,000 years, so this method is not useful for materials older than that. Under exceptional conditions a highly elaborate and time-consuming method is available that can read the age of materials up to 75,000 years, but most archaeological materials cannot meet the strict standards that must be invoked. In all dating using the radiocarbon method there is the possibility of contamination from other materials. Hence researchers must exercise great care in handling the specimen to be measured.

The potassium-argon method is technically similar to radiocarbon dating in that it involves a slow radioactive breakdown process. In this case, however, the breakdown of radioactive potassium-40 (found in volcanic materials and some other rocks) occurs with a half-life of about 1.3 billion years! Using a mass spectrometer it is possible to estimate the ages of materials that are very old. The radioactive potassium-40 breaks down into argon-40, and the ratio of K^{40}/Ar^{40} is computed.

The potassium-argon method of dating made the headlines in the 1960s when Louis S. B. Leakey announced to the world that human fossil materials from Olduvai Gorge in east Africa were nearly two million years old based on potassium-argon dating of the volcanic materials above and below the fossil remains.

The dating of materials occupies an important place in our discussion because so much archaeological analysis depends on establishing the ages of various sites and materials relative to one another. When the archaeologist has established some dates, the task is only begun, however. The modern archaeologist is interested in inferring general social and cultural facts from the material objects left in the ground. For example, if he or she excavates a small village and finds that all the house remains are alike except for one that is much larger, richer, and better furnished, it may be inferred that the larger house represents the dwelling of a chief. On the other hand, if the unusual house floor has numbers of ritual objects in it, it may be suggested that the special occupant was a religious leader. Inferences from archaeological remains allow the archaeologist to study the growth of empires, overthrow of dynasties, development of a middle class, spread of new religions, increasing craft specialization, victories and defeats in warfare, and other important social events. It is easy to see, then, why the archaeologist makes a significant contribution to history, as well as to other fields of study.

Physical Anthropology

"Digging up old skeletons" has been the usual stereotype of fieldwork in physical anthropology, and this is still an important part of that branch of study. One hero among physical anthropologists, Louis S. B. Leakey, spent a large portion of his adult life in searching for human fossil remains in East Africa, accompanied by his wife and co-worker, Mary. Their finds of human remains dating from two million years ago were the fruits of many years of fieldwork. Much of the fieldwork of the physical anthropologist takes the same patterns (digging for and dating remains) that were described for the archaeologist. In fact, they often work together. The main difference between the two areas of study is that the archaeologist seeks information concerning human cultural history, while the physical anthropologist searches for evidence of our biological evolution.

Physical anthropologists also carry out field research on living human communities. In the past this activity often consisted of obtaining measurements of people's height, weight, eye color, hair texture and color, and cephalic index, or skull measurement. The cephalic index, obtained by dividing the width of the skull by its length, was formerly thought to be a very important clue to relationships among the different populations, or "races" of people. More recent investigations have shown, however, that the supposedly fixed and reliable cephalic index can be strongly affected by environment. Some populations that were thought to be long-headed have in some mysterious way become more round-headed, forcing abandonment of that means of "racial" classification.

Revolutionary developments in physical anthropology have produced greatly refined methods of measurement and observation of human physical characteristics. Increasingly, the physical anthropologists are concerned with *internal* characteristics of the human body—components of the blood and other body fluids, measures of body fat (obtained by examining skin folds and through X-rays), blood pressures, growth rates, and many other complex characteristics. Analysis of blood types has been particularly important in recent years, for it has been found that the A-B-O blood types, and many others, lesser-known components of blood, are excellent clues to genetic inheritance, immune processes, and other characteristics.

Physical anthropolgists working in areas of genetics and immunology employ the technological equipment and methods found among other biomedical researchers. Frequently, the physical anthropologists are most interested in the *portable* laboratory equipment that can be taken into remote areas to study the characteristics and physiological adaptations of non-Western populations.

Linguistics

Nineteenth-century linguists had very little equipment to aid them in fieldwork. Having arrived in the community in which he or she intended to study a particular language, the linguist located an informant (someone willing and able to speak to the linguist in the local tongue) and asked him to say particular words and sentences. The linguist simply relied on his own ears to pick up the sounds of the language, which were transcribed into notebooks in the form of phonetic markings—the linguists' own special cross-cultural alphabet. Very often, of course, the linguist also needed an interpreter, unless the informants were bilingual.

The linguist frequently collects information on language in the form of stories—folktales, myths, etc. —so that the professional linguist may be a collector of folklore as well.

Thomas Edison's phonograph (patented in 1877) produced a major revolution in the field methods of linguistics. The year after the phonograph was available to the public, the anthropologist J. W. Fewkes used one to collect forty cylinders of sample vocabularies, folklore texts, conversations, and other materials from the Passamaquoddy Indians in Maine. For the first time, the sounds of the native speaker—his or her own intonations and speech patterns—could be stored away to be played back later as the linguist analyzed the data.

Nineteenth-century linguists generally analyzed languages by analogy with the categories of Latin, the language of scholars. Description of a previously unstudied language involved the search for nouns, adjectives, prepositions, prefixes, suffixes, and other familiar elements of grammar. It was Franz Boas and his students who broke away from the narrow view of Latin grammatical categories and concentrated on description of American Indian languages in terms of their own "natural" grammatical elements.

Linguists have found that each language is a self-contained and unique system for categorizing and talking about experience. Some languages do not even have words in the way we ordinarily think of the word *word*. The Eskimo language, for example, expresses ideas such as "The man stood on the high hill" in clusters of "idea particles" or morphemes, which cannot be separated out into six or seven words, as in the English sentence, but rather are all stuck together in a single "word-sentence."

Although linguists try to describe individual languages in terms of their own intrinsic patterns of grammar and sounds, they make systematic comparisons among languages, searching for "families of languages" descended from common ancestors. The discovery that most of the languages in Europe are descended from a common ancestral Indo-European language was one of the revolutionary developments in linguistics. Related languages are discovered by systematic comparison of their vocabularies for sound-and-meanings correspondences. For example, if *hound* in English refers to a kind of dog, and *hund* in German also refers to "man's best friend," then it is probable that both words are derived from a common ancestral form. Systematic comparison of large numbers of such English-German word pairs provides the evidence that the two languages are related. The linguist's comparative method becomes quite complicated by the fact that all languages change in pronunciation and grammar over the years and centuries. The similarities between German and English are relatively easy to spot, but it is harder to understand how, for example, the Russian word pronounced *adyin* is related to our English word *one*.

The research methods of the linguist, like those of other anthropologists, have been greatly assisted by modern mechanical devices, such as magnetic recorders, sound spectrographs, and electronic computers, but none of these machines make any less complex the painstaking analysis that the researcher must carry out with his or her own brain, eyes, and hands.

Social/Cultural Anthropology

Cultural/social anthropologists usually carry out research by means of fieldwork, often in communities with lifeways quite different from those the anthropologists live in. In the past, ethnographic work was carried out in Africa, the islands of the South Seas, on Indian reservations, or in peasant villages of India, Southeast Asia, or Latin America. Typically such field trips lasted from six months to a year or more, and field expeditions lasting two or three years were not uncommon. Whatever the particular theoretical focus of the researcher, it usually requires several months for the fieldworker to establish good working relations in the community and to learn the local idioms sufficiently well that fieldwork can proceed without language barriers.

Since the mid-sixties, there have been a great many innovations and theoretical discussions concerning fieldwork methods, and ethnologists have become very conscious of questions of methodology. Technological features, including high quality tape recorders, portable videotape equipment, and other equipment, have been added to the fieldwork inventory. Nonetheless the old and the new methods of ethnological fieldwork are all variations around two basic procedures: (1) interviewing local people and (2) observing social and cultural behavior (and products of behavior) through the varieties of "participant observation."

Anthropologist John Lozier in field research, checking some data with his Mexican village informants.

Like the linguist, the social anthropologist seeks out reliable, knowledgeable informants—those people in the community who know the most about the life of the community and are the most willing to tell what they know. In some communities nearly everyone is willing to talk about the local way of life; in other places the anthropologist must work hard to establish enough trust so that even one or two people will consent to give extensive information. Again, like the linguist, the anthropologist must often hire an interpreter, unless he or she has learned the local language beforehand. Nowadays, in increasing numbers of societies there are bilinguals whose second language is English or French or Spanish. But most anthropologists seek to learn the local language during their fieldwork period—even if fieldwork is possible in the anthropologist's own language. The reasons for the anthropologist's interest in language are three-fold: (1) most people feel increasing closeness and trust toward those outsiders who make an attempt to learn their language; (2) the anthropologist who does not speak the local language misses much information because he or she does not understand conversations going on around him or her; (3) frequently the social meanings of particular elements of human behavior are poorly expressed in translated form, and one cannot get an adequate understanding of them, except in the native tongue.

The experiences of anthropologists and others have taught that even in a small community any one informant does not know all about life in that community, nor is a particular individual, however well-informed, always accurate in telling what he or she knows. Almost any informant in a small town probably knows how many police officers and doctors there are. Most informants know which local stores have what commodities. But few informants can be uniformly reliable in matters of what townspeople eat for supper, what they think about outsiders, where people go for medical care, and so on. Therefore, the anthropologist tries to locate and use the services of a number of different informants who occupy diverse positions in the local community, interviewing individuals from different family groups, neighborhoods, social classes, and other major sub-units of the local society. The information given by these various individuals can be cross-checked for accuracy. Often the upper-class members of a village are not well informed on the details of behavior of lower-class individuals, and vice versa.

Even the best informants, cross-checked against one another, provide the anthropologist with a very distilled, inadequate picture of life in a society. A local inhabitant might be completely unconscious of, or take for granted, and thus not mention, aspects of culture that would have great significance to the outside observer. Much of the richness of information the anthropologist wants can be obtained only by "participant observation"—the participation by the researcher in the activities themselves. The anthropologist hopes to be so accepted in the regular life of the community that he or she can be present and take part in crop planting, religious ceremonies, initiation rites, weddings and wakes, as well as the day-to-day routines of social interaction—visiting, gossiping, games, and other recreation in the community.

As participant observer the anthropologist tries to accomplish several major objectives. First, he or she hopes, by being involved rather extensively in the local life, to gain the respect and trust of the local people, so that they will feel confident enough to reveal aspects of their private lives. Second, participation is often the best way to see the complex details of human behavior. A Pueblo rain-making ceremony, for example, cannot be fully described by an informant, however eloquent he or she may be. It has to be seen by the anthropologist in order to "get the full picture." Having seen the ceremony, she or he can then ask intelligent questions about it for fuller understanding. Third, the anthropologist often finds that the *emotional* meaning of a particular human activity does not become clear until he or she has experienced the activity first hand. The anthropologist, thus, is an investigator who wants to find out how it "feels" to take part in a food-gathering expedition, to dance all night in a harvest festival, or to sit in a darkened room watching and listening to the performance of a gifted shaman curing a sick person.

Sometimes the anthropologist's children are important assistants in fieldwork.

The Patterning of Behavior

Common-sense experience tells us that the ways of life of most people include some patterns of behavior, or "customs," that are highly predictable and regular, so that no full-scale survey or poll is necessary to establish certain kinds of generalizations. Such highly patterned "customs" include the following:

1. The people of Cedar Rapids use knives and forks to eat their meals.
2. English motorists drive on the left side of the road.
3. Traffic stops at red lights and moves forward when the traffic lights turn green.
4. The national anthem is played before the start of football games.

In small-scale societies—especially those with many traditional features—there may be a fairly large number of such behavior patterns that are, practically speaking, 100 percent predictable. Furthermore, in any community, traditional or modern, there are many geographic featues and technological devices that require certain regularized patterns of manipulation or management. The main details in the handling of boats, throwing of the nets and hauling in of fish are likely to be quite predictable from day to day and person to person in a group of Samoan fishing people—as long as they are all using the same equipment. It is not necessary for the anthropologist to take a poll of the participants in order to describe these kinds of regular patterns.

The regular patterning of behavior in all human societies makes it possible for individuals to predict one another's behavior and to interact successfully in cooperative work and a multitude of other activities. Even fights and warfare are generally enacted according to "rules" and customs. The British Redcoats were very angry when they found that the American Revolutionists didn't behave according to accepted European patterns of military behavior!

But recognition of the patterning of behavior has sometimes led anthropologists and others to assume that nonmodern peoples, peasants and tribal societies, are slaves of custom and tradition, with little variation in behavior within local groups. Individuals in such societies who appeared to vary from the "norms" or usual patterns have often been labeled "deviant" or "exceptional," thus preserving the illusion that practically all the people in the tribe or village are pretty much alike.

Ethnological research in recent years has shown us that in all societies, no matter how small and traditional, people vary a good deal in their behavior, personality, opinions, and life-style. There are always differences in family size and composition and skills and interests, and in most societies there are variations in available resources affecting the activities and life-styles of community members. In recent years the rapid pace of modernization, reaching into nearly every corner of the world, has introduced another kind of variation into traditional communities— differential "modernity" or "cosmopoliteness" as some researchers call it. The fact of intracultural, intracommunity variations in people's beliefs and behaviors does not mean that there are no clear patterns; it simply underlines the need for careful *sampling* and cross-checking of information, rather than accepting the stereotypes of a few key informants.

The Anthropologist as "Research Instrument"

Descriptions of people's lifeways as recorded in ethnographic reports usually include statements about the ways the field-worker gleaned the cultural information. Often the ethnographer includes statements about his or her main informants, who they were and how much they contributed to the research, as well as descriptions of the structured interviews and, occasionally, some specialized structured observations (and perhaps archival information) that resulted in statistical statements. Beyond the formal methods of data gathering, every ethnographic study includes a great deal of description based on the field-worker's overall knowledge of the people and their habits. Here are some examples:

> Although some Madangs are tolerant, many are quick to point out differences in custom between themselves and the foreigners and to regard them as inferior.

> A wedding celebration called forth extraordinary efforts on the part of the family, which revealed their traditional orientations and their status.

These generalizations are based on many observations (including people's verbal statements) about which the field-worker presents only anecdotal evidence. Concepts such as "tolerant," "regard them as inferior," "extraordinary efforts," and "reveal their traditional orientations," are presumably based on the well-informed theoretical training of the anthropologist. The reader must, in effect, trust the accuracy and objectivity (and theoretical sophistication) of the anthropologist, as an "expert witness" about the community he or she studied.

In some instances, however, ethnographic generalizations that seemed credible at first have later been sharply challenged—either because of changes in theoretical perspectives or because another field researcher went to the same area and found (or claimed to find) that things weren't exactly the way the earlier researcher had said they were. One of the well-known anthropological debates that arose from such differences of perspective concerned the now-famous town of Tepoztlán in central Mexico. Robert Redfield had studied the community in the 1920s and described the people in quite idyllic, "at-one-with-the-universe" terms. Seventeen years later Tepoztlán was studied intensively by Oscar Lewis and a team of field-workers. They produced a much more mixed report, emphasizing conflict, factionalism, and social inequalities, along with more positive features. Lewis commented about these differences between the two ethnographies, saying of Redfield, "His picture of the village has a Rousseauan quality which glosses lightly over evidence of violence, disruption, curelty, disease, suffering and maladjustment. We are told little of poverty, economic problems, or political schisms ... Our findings, on the other hand, would emphasize the underlying individualism of Tepoztlán institutions and character, the lack of cooperation, the tensions ... "[2].

Redfield answered Lewis, saying, "It is true that the two books describe what might almost seem to be two different peoples occupying the same town ... the greater part of the explanation for the difference between the two reports ... is to be found in differences between the two investigators. ... "

Faced with increasing criticism concerning the looseness of ethnographic documentation, anthropologists have in recent years searched for ways to overcome some of these methodological problems without abandoning altogether the informal and personalized methods that have been the hallmark of fieldwork. Many anthropologists have adopted the use of structured, psychological tests and a variety of other empirical and rigorous methods for *portions* of their fieldwork.

Michael Robbins and associates used a mixture of quantified methods and qualitative, descriptive work in the study of modernization in a series of communities in Uganda. Concerning use of alcoholic beverages, for example, their descriptions included much qualitative data, such as:

> ...*Mwenge* (banana beer) is a customary sacrament in numerous traditional rituals and ceremonies. Libations of *mwenge* are used to consecrate new home and garden sites... *Mwenge* also plays a significant customary role in several ceremonies such as birth and naming ceremonies ... etc.[4]

On the other hand, Robbins went on to test a specific hypothesis that when alcohol is well integrated into the sociocultural system its positive social and physiological functions will tend to outweigh its role as a means of assuaging personal psychological problems. He and his co-workers administered a structured interview to a random sample of seventy-six adults in the research communities, asking about quantity and frequency of drinking, attitudes toward and perceptions of various alcoholic beverages, and other questions.

The structured, statistically analyzed research data provided support for the hypothesis; but the utilization of a random sample also greatly enhanced the general credibility of Robbins' observations about the patterns of alcohol use. That is, the ethnographic description (including statistical analysis) made it quite clear that the field-workers had *not* simply relied on a few casual observations of drinking behavior.

In addition to structured interviews with random samples, ethnographers have also used a variety of other quantifiable information-gathering methods. How would one establish a really credible, comprehensive approximation of the time people spend in various different activities in a nonliterate community? Allen and Orna Johnson asked this question during fieldwork in a tropical South American culture, the Machiguenga people, who make their living from hunting and gathering and small-scale cultivation of crops. To make a satisfactory estimate of male-female division of labor, and related questions of work patterns, the Johnsons constructed a random sample method for visiting each of thirteen households. Each day the randomly designated household was visited at a randomly selected hour to determine what activities all the adult members of the household were engaged in. (Information about the activities were from direct observation plus inquiries concerning household members not presently visible at the house.) During several months they collected a total of 3,495 "spot checks" on 134 different days. Analyzing these "spot checks," they were able to say with strong confidence that women spent more time in manufacturing activities than did men (16 percent as compared with 10 percent of sampled observations), whereas men were engaged in garden labor activities 18.5 percent of the times noted, in comparison with the womens' contribution of 6.6 percent. Both males and females were observed to be idle in approximately equal amounts, (males 18 percent; females 19 percent).[5]

Some ethnographers have devised systems for directly observing behavior. For example, in the "six cultures" study by a Harvard-Cornell team of researchers, samples of children were observed in selected behavior settings in five-minute segments of time.

> ...the observers first mapped the daily routine of boys and girls in the two age groups. They followed the children around, noting their presence in different settings at different times of the day. They recorded the activities in progress in these settings and supplemented their observations by interviews with the adults and the children.[6]

Based on this systematic plan each child in the sample was observed at least fourteen times. A local bilingual research assistant was on hand to translate the verbal interaction. The carefully recorded behavior observations were then coded into a series of content categories. Some examples follow:[7]

	Code Category
Romulo and friend wrestle; both laugh.	"assaults sociably"
Shirley to girl next to her, "Move over."	"seeks dominance"
Barbara to the observer, "I have a pad that's way bigger than that one!"	"seeks attention"

From these carefully coded behavioral observations the Whitings and their associates were able to make generalizations about frequencies of aggressive behavior, differences among children in responses to friendly communications, and other patterns.

Cameras, Videotapes, and Other Research Equipment

To an increasing extent anthropologists have been using technical equipment to improve and systematize field observations. Margaret Mead and Gregory Bateson and colleagues used extensive photographic documentation in research among the Balinese people many years ago,[8] and more recently Sorenson and Gajdusek[9] have photographed extensive footage of behavior—especially behavior of children—in order to record the motor patterns of non-Westernized peoples (e.g., in New Guinea) before they lose their traditional behavioral styles to the rapid spread of Euro-American modernization.

Videotapes have been extensively used in urban research in the United States, as well as in a number of other settings, now that TV equipment at moderate cost has become accessible.

Marvin Harris and associates carried out an ambitious, long-term videotaping of inner-city families in New York City, during which the families were paid for allowing the videotape cameras to be placed in their homes. (They were allowed to turn off the cameras at any time they wished for privacy.) Analysis of food behavior by A. L. DeHavenon showed that there were systematic patterns of "food access" domestic authority and "compliance" within the families. She also found that the people's reports of diet and eating behavior in interviews did not check out with what was actually observed on the videotapes.

Use of videotapes in research is expensive and tedious, but it gives ethnographers a special vantage point, something like that TV viewers get in sports telecasts. In the replays we can second guess the referees and the players about "what really happened!"

The rapid growth of an ecological, energy-and-resources perspective in anthropology has led to occasional use of some other technological research methods. In research in the Machiguenga community mentioned earlier, Montgomery and Johnson used technical equipment to measure the amounts of energy expended by individuals in such activities as hunting, cultivating, and other activities: "A Max Planck respirometer (Model 59) and a portable, micro-fuel-cell powered Teledyne oxygen analyzer (Model 331B) were used.[10]

The researchers were able to persuade a small sample of individuals to carry out regular daily activities with the respirometer equipment strapped on, so that amounts of calories expended could be calculated directly from oxygen consumption. They found the following mean energy expenditures per minute[11] for some sample activities:

	Calories/Minute
Man walking up forest pathways (very hilly terrain)	8.9
Man felling large trees	7.6
Man harvesting maize	5.3
Man making bow and arrow	2.7
Woman planting root crops	2.9
Woman beating cotton	1.9
Woman catching fish with hands	3.1
Woman weaving	1.8
Woman straining manioc	1.9

These are a few examples of the ways in which modern day anthropologists have been adding sophistication and rigor to their methods of data collection. In practically all cases, the quantified and highly structured means of observation are intermingled with the open-ended informal ways of participant observation and other time-tested, personalized ways of getting information. Anthropologists have not given up the earlier ethnographic methods, but they are now supplemented, where feasible, with more rigorous quantifiable research.

In general, modern anthropological research shows increasing care in the presentation of evidence that can be independently examined and evaluated by other researchers.

Synthesis of Anthropological Data

The heightened sophistication of anthropological field-workers and the search for more objective research tools has greatly increased the usefulness of ethnographic reports brought back from the field. At the same time, more attention is now given to the search for more accurate and useful historical and scientific generalizations from the information that is already available about hundreds of societies.

One important development is the refinement of the cross-cultural (statistical) method for examining anthropological generalizations. Some anthropologists attempted cross-cultural studies decades ago, but this type of study has only recently begun to demonstrate its usefulness. Reasons for this success would appear to lie in the greatly increased numbers and quality of primary ethnographic reports, greater sophistication in formulation of questions for theoretical research, and improved methods of rapid collating of information, including use of electronic computers.

In earlier times, any anthropologist who wanted to find some piece of information from a sample of, say, sixty societies around the world, would have to read the individual field reports on all the cases in the sample. After laboriously searching through these individual works, he or she might still learn that much of the needed information was missing. Since World War II, largely due to the efforts of George P. Murdock and his associates, the *Human Relations Area Files* (HRAF) has been established, in which information from hundreds of societies, from all the culture areas of the world, has been abstracted and assembled onto cards that are filed according to a master indexing system. For example, anyone wishing to find information on types of games played in societies around the world can go to the files, locate the appropriate index number, and gather together the required information in a fraction of the time it would have taken to go to the original ethnographic sources. The HRAF files are now available at many universities in the United States.

Using data from the Human Relations Area Files, cross-cultural researchers have tested theoretical hypotheses, for example, about relationships between ways of making a living (hunting-gathering, cultivation, etc.) and a large number of variables such as child training, attitudes toward supernaturals, types of family arrangements, and alcohol use. This statistical cross-cultural research has been very useful in eliminating certain myths and stereotypes from anthropological literature. The research has reduced the degree to which social scientists as well as popular generalizers have "gotten away with" using single, individual cultures to make sweeping statements about "primitive peoples."

One of the more interesting and ambitious cross-cultural research projects is a comprehensive study, by Alan Lomax and associates, of the singing and instrumental music in a large sample of societies around the world. The researchers coded the music of different cultures in terms of "complexity of songs," "degree of embellishment," "repetitiousness of songs," "wordiness of songs," "varying uses of melodic intervals," "counterpoint," and other musical characteristics. They then examined these musical variables in relation to their social variables. They found, for example, that wordiness of songs tends to increase with the degree of social complexity in human communities. Figure 2 illustrates this statistical relationship.[12]

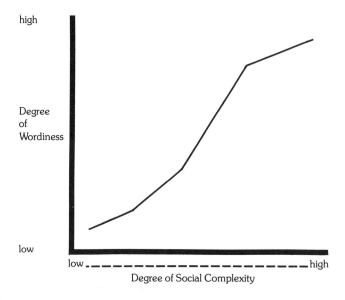

Figure 2.

Although the cross-cultural statistical method has added a significant dimension to theory building in anthropology, theorists do not rely solely on these statistical-techniques in their research synthesis. Much of the direction in systematic analysis of ethnological data involves an interweaving of cross-cultural analysis with intensive study *within* individual societies, or small groups of societies. Thus, some researchers prefer to base their generalizations on intensive analysis of the range of variation in areas of modernization, especially where "more traditional" communities can be compared systematically with the "modernizing" communities of the region.

An excellent example of this kind of regional comparative research is the Culture and Ecology Project carried out by Walter Goldschmidt and associates in East Africa during the 1960s. They made systematic studies in a series of cultural groups, each of which had both pastoralist, cattle-herding communities and sedentary, farming people. Using a mixture of quantified statistical data and general ethnographic description, they found that there were certain systematic differences between the pastoralist peoples and the sedentary farmers, regardless of their cultural identities. Farmers in all the groups tended to be more hostile and suspicious as well as "more indirect, abstract, given to fantasy, more anxious, less able to deal with their emotions, and less able to control their impulses. The herders, on the contrary, are direct, open, bound to reality, and their emotions, though constricted, are under control."[13]

Summary

In all phases of anthropological research there has been a great increase in the use of technical equipment: recording devices, photographic equipment, X-ray devices, sound spectrographs, and electronic computers. In the nonmechanized procedures of gathering data—in interviewing, "observing-while-participating," and digging—anthropologists have become much more sensitive to the necessity for rigorous, accurate description of the observations that lie behind ethnographic generalizations. There has been a great increase in use of statistics in the analysis of certain kinds of anthropological data. Generalizations that used to be regarded as unquestioned facts have been re-examined. Anthropology has become, in many respects, more scientifically respectable. It is probable that anthropology will continue to combine some of the descriptive, holistic methods of the humanities with the more analytic and statistically oriented practices of the social sciences.

Notes

1. Frank Hole and Robert F. Heizer, *An Introduction to Prehistoric Archaeology,* 3rd ed. (New York: Holt, Rinehart and Winston, 1973), P. 45.

2. Oscar Lewis, *Life in a Mexican Village: Tepoztlan Revisited* (Urbana: University of Illinois Press, 1963), pp. 428-29.

3. Robert Redfield, *The Little Community/Peasant Society and Culture* (Chicago: University of Chicago Press, 1970), pp. 134-35.

4. Michael C. Robbins, "Problem Drinking and the Integration of Alcohol in Rural Baganda," *Medical Anthropology* 1 (1977): 1-24.

5. Allen Johnson, "Time Allocation in a Machiguenga Community." *Ethnology* 14 (1975): 301-310.

6. Beatrice Whiting and John Whiting, *Children of Six Cultures: A Psychocultural Analysis* (Cambridge, Mass.: Harvard University Press, 1975), p. 40.

7. Ibid., pp. 187-96.

8. Margaret Mead and Francis C. MacGregor, *Growth and Culture: A Photographic Study of Balinese Children* (New York: Putnam, 1951), based on the photographs of Gregory Bateson.

9. E. Richard Sorenson and Dr. Carleton Gajdusek, *The Study of Child Behavior and Development in Primitive Cultures,* Supplement to *Pediatrics* 37, no. 1 (1966) (Part 2).

10. Edward Montgomery and Allen Johnson, "Machiguenga Energy Expenditure," *Ecology of Food and Nutrition* 6 (1978): 97-105.

11. Ibid.

12. Alan Lomax, *Folk Song Style and Culture* (Washington, D.C.: American Association for the Advancement of Science, 1968).

13. Walter Goldschmidt et al., "Variation and Adaptability of Culture: A Symposium," *American Anthropologist* 67 (1965): 400-447.

Recommended Reading

Hester, Thomas, Robert Heizer, and John Graham. *Field Methods in Archaeology* (Palo Alto: Mayfield, 1975).

This book presents a comprehensive, readable description of archaeological research, written by scholars with many years of experience in field research. The coverage ranges from mapping and recording of excavation data, to methods of chronological inference and classification.

Gudschinsky, S. *How To Learn an Unwritten Language* (New York: Holt, Rinehart and Winston, 1967).

Gudschinsky's small handbook is an interesting and quite readable introduction to methods of linguistic research.

Birdsell, J.B. *Human Evolution*, 2nd edition (Chicago: Rand McNally, 1975).

While the details of research methods in physical anthropology are not the primary focus of Birdsell's discussion, he provides an exciting range of materials concerning the steps of inference physical anthropologists employ in understanding the fossil record of human evolution.

Pelto, Pertti J. and Gretel H. Pelto. *Anthropological Research: the Structure of Inquiry* (New York: Cambridge University Press, 1978).

Although this book includes a chapter devoted to the "art and science of field work," it is much more a guide to the conceptual research tools (interviews, standardized observations, tests) and the logic of hypothesis-testing in anthropological research. Field work in anthropology in this analysis is a complex interweaving of numerical and non-numerical methods.

four

Significant Research
in Anthropology

Few people would deny that the study of humankind is concerned with phenomena of great complexity. In fact, many critics of the social sciences have claimed that human behavior is essentially beyond effective scientific study. According to this line of argument, the influence of our "free will" and the enormous, apparently unlimited possibilities for variations in human behavior make the efforts of generalizing about nature and culture essentially fruitless, if not dangerous. To make matters worse, there is the inevitable subjectivity of studying ourselves—a problem not encountered by the physical scientists in their study of atoms, animals, and astrophysics.

Critics of the social sciences (including anthropology) can point to "conflicting facts," inconsistencies in terminology, and the seemingly hopeless divergences in theoretical assumptions as evidence of the obvious immaturity of these studies. Usually skeptics point out the contrast to the great precision and elaborate mathematics found in physics and chemistry. They are quick to mention advances in communications systems, automation of industry, and, more recently, space technology as evidence of progress in the "real sciences"—progress that they believe the social sciences can never match. In comparison with the precision achieved in sending a manned flight to the moon, the scientific study of humankind seems most chaotic.

Anthropology, like the other social sciences, is a rather young discipline, and every field of scholarship must pass through a relatively long stage of growing up. The formative period of a science must involve collecting descriptive information, trial-and-error testing of methods and theories (with inevitable fads or temporary explorations), organization of preliminary classifications of "types" of subjects to be studied, and many other steps. In the later mature phase, general principles and scientific laws can be developed. Much current anthropological study is still in the data-gathering and exploratory phases. However, the gathering of descriptive information about human history and peoples of the world is no small achievement in itself, and this store of information, once gathered, can be put to a variety of uses.

In this chapter we will consider some of the major areas of research endeavor in contemporary anthropology.

The Evidence of Human Evolution

Some of our tool-using "ape-human" ancestors were living in East Africa almost three million years ago. A series of fossil discoveries during the early and middle 1960s, mainly the work of Louis S. B. Leakey, his wife Mary, and son Richard, sharply revised our picture of human biological evolution, adding further evidence to the general progression from ape to human. The accumulation of new fossil material over the past two decades has steadily expanded the evidence concerning the two-million-years-plus of human biological evolution, and it has steadily pushed back the point of "earliest beginnings" of human cultural capability. Cultural capability in this instance means evidence of purposeful making and use of tools.

The new technological breakthrough that established firmly the evidence of our antiquity was the potassium-argon method of radiological dating. Establishing firm dates for those ancient fossils gives an added confidence to the emerging picture of our human beginnings. In 1974 to 1976 important new fossil discoveries in East Africa included a relatively complete skull nearly 2.9 million years old. This skull is remarkable because it is much more "modern looking" than any other known fossil of similar age.

The discoverer of these important new materials was Richard Leakey, son of the late L. B. Leakey, whose finds in the 1960s brought worldwide attention. The newest materials from East Africa continue to support the belief of the Leakeys (both senior and junior) that a genus *Homo*—a large brained direct ancestor of our modern humanity—was living in East Africa contemporaneously with at least two other erect-walking apelike competitors. Thus, there may have been as many as three different species of erect-walking animals in East and South Africa, all of them with bigger brains than modern apes.

The name *Australopithecus* has been given to a large collection of fossils found in dozens of locations in Africa. These creatures stood about four feet tall and had rather humanlike faces and teeth compared to animals like the chimpanzee and gorilla. One branch, or variety, of *Australopithecus* ("southern ape") seems to have been vegetarian, with large grinding teeth suitable for that kind of diet. The other *Australopithecus* species, and *Homo habilis,* were apparently omnivores with a diet that included a variety of small animals as well as nuts, fruits, seeds, and other vegetable materials.

The fossil evidence concerning human evolution demonstrates a series of gradual changes from small "ape-humans" of three million years ago. Growth of brain size was one of the main developments. Figure 3 compares brain sizes of various fossil specimens, as well as modern humans, chimpanzees, and gorillas.

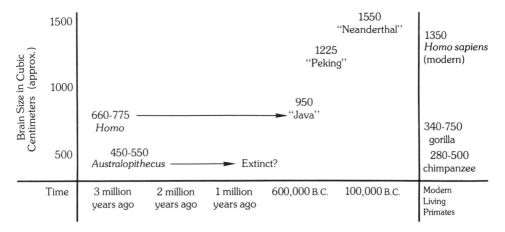

Figure 3.

The processes of natural selection, as postulated by Charles Darwin, have acted thousands of generations to produce a human animal with distinct and very special capabilities. From the fossil evidence we can "read" these processes in broad outline:

1. doubling or tripling of brain capacity (see fig. 3).
2. development of fully upright posture, with skull balanced on top of spinal column, and straight leg bones, and
3. refinement of hand structure for fine-grained, precise manipulation.

The *Australopithecus* ape-humans apparently became extinct at least half a million years ago, leaving the most "successful" of the trio—the large brained genus *Homo* to carry on the line of evolution leading to modern humans. Many researchers have made suggestions about what happened to *Australopithecus*. Perhaps they simply didn't develop brains (and hands) refined enough to cope with the large numbers of predators (lions, leopards, cheetahs) and other dangers of Africa. Perhaps their mortal enemies were larger brained, more capable *Homo* creatures, who were more flexible in dietary habits and perhaps somewhat more aggressive as well.

The Java fossils, first discovered in the 1890s, show that our ancestors had spread to the Far East by about 600,000 years ago. Further evidence for this geographical spreading of genus *Homo* came in the 1920s with the discovery of a large number of skeletal remains in a cave near Peking in China. The Peking fossils are in many ways similar to the Java remains, but the brains are somewhat bigger, and they were found with clear evidence of tool using as well as the oldest evidence of purposeful use of fire. From time to time the Peking fossils have received special coverage on television—mainly because of the continued mystery of their disappearance during World War II.

That first Neanderthal specimen is now believed to be representative of the later stages of human evolution, dating from a more 50,000 to 150,000 years ago. Neanderthal-like fossils have been found in Germany, France, Spain, Italy, Belgium, Israel, Africa, and in Southeast Asia. These large brained animals, technically labelled *Homo sapiens neanderthalensis,* were big-game hunters with complex cultural capabilities—capable of making a living from hunting-and-gathering during the brutally cold and difficult periods of the later Ice Ages.

Fossil skeletons closely resembling modern *Homo sapiens sapiens* have been found from deposits in Europe, Africa, and Asia that are at least 30,000 to 40,000 years old. There is still debate among anthropologists on the question of whether our modern *Homo sapiens* are *direct* descendants of Neanderthal, versus the theory that Neanderthal, with the heavy brow ridges and massive skulls, was a sidebranch that somehow got eliminated in the competition, just a few dozen millenia before modern times. The curious puzzle about the Neanderthals, whether direct ancestor or a side branch, is that their brain sizes averaged a bit larger than modern *Homo sapiens sapiens!* Perhaps we developed more complex, streamlined brain organization and didn't need quite such big heads. Electronic computers and CB radios are not the only things in which there has been improvement in the circuitry.

The fossil record of human evolution, from three million years ago down to modern times, is a story that seems to have its earliest beginnings in Africa, followed by spread to Asia and Europe. Our ancestors were in all three continents over a half a million years ago, if not earlier. The fossil evidence of humans in the New World— North and South America—is quite recent. The ancestors of American Indians and Inuit (Eskimo) came to the Americas by way of Siberia perhaps 50,000 years ago. But the earliest Americans were already modern *Homo sapiens sapiens* in their biological makeup. There were no ape-humans in the Western Hemisphere.

The Evidence of Human Cultural Evolution

Some of those same sites in East Africa—in Ethiopia and Tanzania—in which the Leakeys and other researchers have found the fossils, also have abundant evidence of culture in the form of stone tools, broken animal bones, and in one instance a ring of stones that may have been a rude shelter. The stone tools are crudely chipped from pebbles, and would probably be unnoticed if they were found in a gravel driveway. Identification of their "tool" status depends on *where* they were found (sometimes right with the skeletal remains) and careful analysis of the patterning of chipping.

For several million years our ancestors apparently lived as small bands of foragers and hunters, using only very simple stone, bone, and wooden weapons and implements. Very few important changes occurred in the cultural equipment of the genus *Homo* during those first millions of years, as far as can be determined from archaeological research. The rich stores of stone tools that constitute our main evidence for that long period in cultural history show a very gradual refinement and specialization in equipment—from crude pebble-tools to carefully shaped handaxes like the ones found by Boucher de Perthes in the gravels near Paris 150 years ago.

Archaeological excavations in western Europe provide evidence of significant development of cultural complexity near the end of the Ice Age. During the last

40,000 years of the Great Glaciation, the "cave people" who roamed what is now France and Spain developed a style in their cave paintings and other art work that still today ranks among our greatest artistic achievements. On the walls of nearly inaccessible underground caverns they painted amazing polychromatic representations of the mammoths, bison, reindeer, and other animals that they hunted. It is generally believed that these master works were produced for the practical purposes of hunting magic and ritual, rather than representing *l'art pour l'art*.

The truly revolutionary changes in human culture that make our complex modern life possible developed during the past 10,000 years—a tiny fraction of our total cultural history. The series of inventions that radically changed our way of living centered on the domestication of plants and animals. Excavations by Robert Braidwood and others in Iraq, Iran, and Israel have given us a much better picture of the probable beginnings of the "food-production revolution." Archaeological and botanical evidence strongly favors the Near East as one probable "birthplace" of agriculture, for many of the plants that humans have learned to sow, care for, and harvest grow wild in that part of the world. In some sites in the same area, archaeologists have found stone "sickles" that were probably used for harvesting the wild plants in a time before people discovered ways to plant and cultivate crops for themselves.

Braidwood and his associates have carried out systematic investigations of the site of an ancient hillside village in Iraq.[1] This village, called Jarmo, appears to have been a cluster of about twenty-five mud houses. The people who lived there grew barley and wheat and kept some domestic animals but also relied a great deal upon wild foods as well. These people, and people of similar ancient villages of the Near East, may have been the not-so-far-removed descendants of the first cultivators in that region. From radiocarbon samples the remains of the village have been dated back about 8,500 years.

Little agricultural villages like Jarmo may have been only one or two steps removed from the hunting-and-foraging way of life, but those are mighty steps. Controlling their own food supply to a much greater degree than was possible for Stone Age hunters, these people could live in settled villages and could support a larger population.

The increased food production made possible by domestication of plants and animals did not necessarily lead to any new leisure time. In fact there is now evidence from several modern hunter-gatherer groups that pre-agricultural people often have more leisure and more adequate diets than many people with crops and domestic animals. But the surpluses of food and new social arrangements made possible from domesticated food sources promoted new kinds of craftsmanship, including the making of pottery, basketry, woven products (from the wool of the animals), and other manufacturing.[2]

New evidence from archaeological sites in northern Thailand supports the likelihood that domesticated plants and animals, and settled patterns of living, developed independently in Southeast Asia. Chester Gorman, as well as other researchers, have found evidence of prehistoric cultivation of taro, yams, and other tropical vegetables. The diet of the people included water chestnuts, cucumbers, peppers, almonds, as well as fish, pork and venison. Some of the vegetable foods may have been gathered wild, but the overall picture is one of at least partial cultivation supplementing, or supplemented by, hunting and gathering. In any case some of the materials from the site, called Spirit Cave, date from 11,000 years ago. There are some other recently discovered remains in the same region that point to a developed pattern of food production that may be even earlier than the rise of cultivation and sedentary life in the Near East.

A third major area of plant domestication developed independently in the Americas, from Mexico to Peru. This development took place later than the domestication of plants and animals in the Old World, although there is evidence of some domesticated foods from about 6500-7000 B.C. The first cultivated plants in America were very different from the inventory of crops in the Old World. Gourds, beans, squash, chili peppers, and then corn (maize) became the domestic food sources for the ancient peoples in Mexico, millenia before the rise of the Aztecs. A major piece of the archaeological evidence for these developments is from the Valley of Tehuacan, where Richard MacNeish for the Peabody Foundation for Archaeology has carried out extensive excavations over a number of years. [3]

Archaeologists doing research in Mexico and Peru are often confronted with an embarrassment of riches. The prehistoric Indian peoples built extensive cities with monumental architecture on a par with ancient Rome and biblical Babylon. Many of these New World archaeological wonders have only recently been explored in more thorough scientific fashion, even though their impressive monuments have long been tourist attractions.

The city of Tula, north of Mexico City, was the seat of the Toltec empire. These massive colonnades, depicting warriors, stand 15 feet high, and perhaps once held up the roof of a sacred temple.

Archaeologists may yet find that there have been other centers where agricultural ways of life originated. One candidate is West Africa. There is some evidence for an early florescence of foodgrowing that may turn out to be independent of the developments in the Near East. In any case, from those first centers of domestication the ideas, techniques, and products of a new way of food production spread, over the centuries, to other parts of the world. The Near East patterns of agriculture with wheat, barley, sheep, cattle, goats, and pigs spread widely into Europe, Asia, and Africa. In the Americas the corn-beans-squash complex of foods (with very little support from domestic animal foods) spread by slow degrees north and south—a process that was still going on in North America when the first Europeans arrived. In South America the food production complex included potatoes, which became a major food source along the western side of the South American continent, especially in Peru where the Incas built up a vast empire a few centuries before the arrival of European conquerors.

The change from hunting and gathering to domesticated food production had very great consequences for human lifeways. Once settled food-producing communities were established, processes were set in motion that led to larger and larger populations, more and more social complexity and social inequality, and the invention of new kinds of technical equipment. Compared to the millions of years of hunting and gathering, it took only a few thousand years to generate the present-day urban-industrial system.

The transition to settled, crop-growing communities was undoubtedly a gradual process in many areas. Hunting-gathering people did not necessarily find it a vast improvement to stay around a home base, cultivating crops and tending domesticated animals. In fact, crop failure must have been frequent then, as it is today, and there are other negative features (e.g., in sanitation and health) that come with settling down in permanent houses.

Archaeological evidence concerning the earliest settled communities continues to point to the Near East, in the areas where the domestication of food crops developed rapidly in that period 10,000 to 12,000 years ago. The walled town of Jericho was one of the very earliest large settlements. Archaeologists estimate that the town covered about 10 acres and had a population of perhaps 2000 people. The location of this oasis in a mostly dry area suggests that Jericho was in a controlling position in the Dead Sea salt trade. The massive walls around the town, nearly 20 feet high, suggest that defending valuable property from the outside world, had become a problem.

Another well developed settlement grew up at Çatal Hüyük in southern Turkey, probably as a trade center with control over valuable obsidian in the nearby mountains. Growing up around 8000—9000 years ago, Çatal Hüyük in its developed phase covered over 30 acres, with impressive ceremonial buildings, clay figurines, wall paintings, and other marks of artistic and craft activities. [4]

The world's first cities, some of them mentioned in the Old Testament, were built in the fertile valleys of the Tigris and Euphrates rivers. Tremendous archaeological work has gone into uncovering the evidence about the transition from little farming villages like Jarmo to the concentration of people in cities such as Al Ubaid, out of which grew Sumarian civilization. The cities were made possible by the invention of irrigation works in the river valleys, and it appears that those earliest cities were governed by theocracies of priests who controlled secular activities of food production and handicrafts, as well as sacred ritual activities.

Evidence unearthed so far indicates that the first cities developed about 4000 B.C. The evidence also shows that about the same time, striking new techniques and implements were invented by the people of the Mesopotamian region. Extraction and use of metals was invented, the making of bronze from a combination of tin and

Table 2. *The History of Human Cultural and Biological Evolution (read from the bottom up)*

Time (approx.)	Old World	New World
Now		Aztec and Incan empires Mayan Civilization
Birth of Christ		
2,000 B.C.	Rise of Greek Civilization	Beginnings of Mayan towns
	Invention of metal-working, writing, and many other new things	
4,000 B.C.	First cities in Mesopotamia	Invention of maize growing in Middle America
	(Catal Hüyük) Walled town of Jericho	
10,000 B.C.	Invention of grain-growing in Near East	
	Spirit Cave in Southeast Asia, early food cultivation	
	Western European cave art	
	Many new forms of stone tools	
100,000 B.C.	Neanderthal	First humans arrive in New World (by way of Alaska)
	Well-designed handaxes found widely in Old World	
500,000-600,000 B.C.	Java and Peking fossils (and many stone tools)	
1 million B.C.	Crude stone tools in many areas of Africa, Asia, Europe	
1.7-2.9 million B.C.	*Australopithecus* and *Homo habilis* with stone tools at Olduvai Gorge and other sites in East Africa	

copper was developed, craftspeople began to do remarkably good work in the manufacture of weapons, ornaments, tools, pottery, and other goods, and the record-keepers for the priestly temples began to use more complicated marks for recording grain receipts and other transactions. The first written language and mathematics came into being. The servants of the temples also developed accurate means of keeping track of the seasons by observing the movements of heavenly bodies. Astronomy, the oldest science, came into being, and with it, the first calendars.

The inventions and discoveries of the Mesopotamians spread widely in the Old World. From the archaeological evidence it appears likely that the ancient civilizations of Egypt, India, and even China were the result of the diffusion of strategic inventions—agriculture, metal-working, and record-keeping—from the original cradle of civilization, Mesopotamia.

The influence of Mesopotamian civilization apparently had very little to do with the rise of Mayan, Aztec, and Incan civilizations of the New World. The archaeological materials tell the story of an independent development, involving a set of inventions and discoveries different from those of the Near East. Quite different foods were cultivated, and metal-working, writing, mathematics, calendars, astronomy, and other achievements appear to have been developed out of local traditions, rather than being carried from the distant civilizations of Mesopotamia and Egypt. The remarkable achievements of the American Indians took place several thousand years later than similar growth in the Near East. In fact, much of the growth of Middle American and Mayan civilizations took place within the past 2,000 years. A summary of the main developments in the history of human culture is presented in table 2.

The Data on Human Behavior

The masses of information that anthropologists have collected about the peoples of the world always point in two directions. Looking backward, we are naturally interested in tracing our biological and cultural history, as outlined above. The same information, however, is also the raw material from which we seek to put together generalizations about human behavior. We want to understand modern human behavior in all its forms, rather than merely to learn some interesting facts about the past.

Now, if a biologist were searching for generalizations about the behavior of birds, it is unlikely that he or she would rely upon data limited to descriptions of the behavior of birds of North America. Similarly, no sensible oceanographer attempts to study the characteristics of the oceans using only information from the North Atlantic. These scientists search out the fullest possible information from all parts of our globe when pursuing study of their favorite subject. It therefore seems strange to anthropologists that there have been so many studies made and books written about human nature, religion, law, art, and other aspects of human culture using information from one small group of humans; namely, Americans and Europeans.

The tendency of many scholars to generalize about "human nature" from such a narrow sampling of the available evidence appears to be due to two main factors. First, information about the beliefs, institutions, marriage patterns, economic systems, and personalities of the great variety of non-European peoples has not been easily available to everyone. Until about 100 years ago there was no systematically collected mass of ethnographic data. The second, and perhaps more important reason, is that people everywhere tend to view their own way of life as the most reasonable and natural, as exemplary of human behavior at its best. It is not surprising, therefore, that even the most profound philosophers of both East and West have commonly derived their theories of human nature from study of their own countries and neighboring nations, deeming the customs of more distant peoples as savage, quaint, barbaric, illogical, unnatural, or even subhuman.

As early as the seventeenth and eighteenth centuries, however, some European philosophers began to use information about the "Red Indians" and the people of the South Seas as evidence for their theories. Rousseau's use of ethnographic materials for his concept of the "noble savage" is an example of this tendency. The ethnographic information available to these men was, of course, rather scanty and inaccurate, since it had been collected in an unorganized manner by a variety of travelers, adventurers, missionaries, and others, as a sideline to their major activities and interests. The philosophers could hardly draw useful conclusions about human nature when their ethnographic sources told of one-eyed giants, tribes with mouths in the middle of their stomachs, people without either language or religion, and other fantasies.

Only in the twentieth century has the level of ethnographic information so improved that the more striking absurdities have been dropped from common belief, and something approaching accurate descriptions of human lifeways have become available from the important geographical subareas of the world. Even today there are great gaps in the availability of particular kinds of information. To give just one example, only since about 1955 have anthropologists made serious attempts to gather systematic data on nonmodern systems of legal practices.

Widespread recognition among nonanthropologists of the importance of cross-cultural materials for generalizations about human behavior has developed only in the past twenty-five years. Almost anyone writing today on such subjects as religious systems, the human family, personality development, or law-ways, feels compelled to take notice of at least some of the rich store of relevant information from non-Western societies.

Promising Developments in Anthropological Theory

The accumulation of descriptive information about human behavior, past and present, has now reached proportions that make possible significant advances in anthropological theory. One of the perennially favorite topics of anthropological theory has been the question of cultural evolution—the search for general stages or regular patterns in human culture history. After the nineteenth-century version of cultural evolution had been thoroughly discredited, most anthropologists avoided, almost as a kind of supernatual taboo, any examination of cultural evolutions. In more recent times, there have been serious attempts to build new theories on better foundations.

Julian Steward's theory of "multilinear evolution"[5] has provided a basis for newer perspectives. Instead of assuming that human lifeways everywhere advance through similar sequences of progress from "savagery" to "civilization," Steward has searched for more limited parallels among societies developing in *comparable environmental situations.* Looking at the rise of civilizations in Mesopotamia, Egypt, China, Peru, and Middle America, Steward (along with others) has noted that quite similar processes of cultural growth took place in these widely separated circumstances. The "formative period" in each of these areas was marked by development of metallurgy, population growth, expansion of the dominant culture, building of large irrigation works, and appearance of multi-community "state" organization. Stewards's theories suggest that the development of complex societies in other kinds of natural environments (e.g., northern Europe) would be expected to take different patterns from the ones just described. This theoretical framework assumes that cultural processes must be studied as an interaction among environment, social organization, technological inventory, and ideological patterns—acting upon and influencing each other as people adapt to given environments and try to improve their conditions of living.

Archaeologists and sociocultural anthropologists have found significant new areas of theoretical agreement concerning the ways in which environments, new technological items, and other material conditions of life affect other aspects of culture. New technological devices often have profound effects on social organization, including family relationships, formation of special interest groups, and the broader patterns of social organization.

The rise of social stratification, in concert with the growth of food-producing technology and increased population size, has been demonstrated in the archaeological studies of the Mesopotamian, Mayan, Aztec, and Incan civilizations, as well as in other, smaller scale sites. The same patterns have been demonstrated in a variety of cross-cultural studies, based on comparisons of "cultural cases" ranging from hunter-gatherers to simple cultivators to complex societies with plow agriculture. The growth of social inequalities is promoted by several key factors:

1. production systems (especially of food) that permit intensification and "surplus production," from which taxes, rent, and other tribute can be collected by landlords, chiefs and "nobles."
2. monopolizability of food production resources, especially land, scarce water supplies, and other essentials.
3. presence of warfare, which calls for military controls over civilian populations.
4. a constricted environment in which expansion can only happen through conquest of other people. [6]

A number of excellent recent studies have explored in detail the complex interrelationships between people's environmental situations and the social systems that develop around the particular food and energy resources. John Bennett has explored the different adaptations of ranchers and farmers in the varied environmental circumstances of Saskatchewan in Canada. In modern-day systems of western Canada and elsewhere, the adaptations of individuals and families must take into account *local* resources, but they must also make the most of the resources and restrictions from the wider economic and political networks—governmental support programs, tax structures, and the complex commercial contracts through which farm and ranch products are bought and sold. Bennett and his research associates found that:

Water was the... natural resource in shortest supply and the most unevenly distributed by nature. Its chief economic use in the region was to provide irrigation for the raising of forage crops for livestock ... [7]

The best conservationists in (the region) were the operators of enterprises of large scale, particularly the bigger ranches and the Hutterian Brethren. They were able to take care of their resources and keep some of them out of use only because their incomes were sufficient to cover the losses entailed. This is resources conservation by default, so to speak. ... [8]

An ecological study of quite a different scope is A.P. Vayda's study of factors affecting warfare patterns in three groups in Oceania: the Maori of New Zealand, the Iban of Borneo, and the Maring of New Guinea. The warfare activities of some of these Oceanian peoples have often been described as reflecting magical and religious beliefs—they go to war because "their spiritual juice is running low. What they need is a fresh influx of supernatural vigor, not only to strengthen themselves, their crops and their women, but also to fight off evil spirits. . . . "[9] Vayda's analysis shows that the ebb and flow of warfare patterns also reflect perturbations in population balances in relation to local resources and territory. Thus the "magical beliefs about warfare" cannot be viewed as the prime and only cause of the hostilities.

The recent developments in ecological theory do not eliminate the need for understanding the psychological, ideational factors affecting human behavior. In fact, many of the more promising research directions in anthropology help us to understand the complex *interactions* of people's belief systems and psychological processes with the economic and material conditions affecting their lives.

These interactions are significant, for example, in understanding the situations in which magical practices and religious revitalizations arise. A number of recent studies have found that urbanization and "modernization" often lead to *increases* in certain categories of magic, as well as the growth of diverse religious sects and movements.

It was Bronislaw Malinowski who decades ago first clearly suggested and produced evidence for the relationship between magical practices and life's areas of uncertainty.[10] Those pulse-quickening situations in hunting, warfare, ocean sailing, or other activities where technical abilities are insufficient to affect the uncontrollables of weather, wild animals, stormy seas, dangerous enemies—these are the kinds of situations in which people turn to wish-projections in the form of magical practices. Malinowski saw this response to anxiety as a natural attribute of all humans, including

The development of a more sophisticated ecological theory in anthropology has led to more careful study of food production, nutrition, sex roles, and energy expenditure. Peasant women in Mexico, as in most other parts of the world, expend many calories per day transporting burdens. Often they must carry their infants while they work. (top page 60) The worldwide fuel crisis involves more than petroleum. Firewood is an increasingly scarce commodity in many parts of India, Mexico, and elsewhere. (top page 61) This load of maguey (century plant) leaves will provide a passable substitute for wood to cook the tortillas in a Mexican household. (bottom page 61)

both the Trobriand sailor on the high seas and the modern American embarking on unusually difficult action. Everyone does not incline to magical practices to the same degree, but examples from our own modern society support Malinowski's theory. In areas where our abilities and technology are in doubt, in struggles with incurable illnesses, the dangers of warfare, and even in the uncertainties of hard-fought ball games, we "moderns" easily show interest in rabbits' feet, lucky talismans of all sorts, mystical quack medicines, magical avoidance of certain words, and dozens of other little rituals. Religious conversions and visionary experiences also appear related to intense anxieties.

In an excellent study of two West African societies, S. F. Nadel has demonstrated that accusations of witchcraft tend to be leveled at the people in society who are the most anxiety-provoking in their behavior.[11] Among the Nupe people of Nigeria, for example, there is much tension between husbands and wives. The women, who often have more wealth than the men, frequently engage in trading and shopping expeditions away from their families and express their independence in a number of other ways that run counter to the accepted Nupe standards for virtuous and dutiful women. The analysis shows that ambivalence toward women is at least part of the explanation for the fact that females are much more often accused of witchcraft than are males. Furthermore, the accusations of witchcraft may serve to keep the women somewhat under the control of the insecure males, for witchcraft is a serious crime and steps are taken to punish the alleged offenders.

The importance of these findings about magic and witchcraft is greatly increased when we realize that similar phenomena occur in our modern society. Here, however, the "magical" ideas are often translated into twisted beliefs about Communism, fear of fluoridation, scapegoating of minority groups, weird distortions about "what goes on in our universities," and many other puzzling conceptions. From the cross-cultural anthropological evidence as well as from psychological studies, it appears that people who experience fear and frustrations in their daily lives often develop "magical" beliefs about the sources of their problems. They then project the blame onto "witches," who in our modern society may be racial or religious minorities, "Communists and other radicals," "Those atheists at the university," or other handy targets.

Recent anthropological studies have also thrown new light on the forms and variations in social and religious movements. During the 1950s A.F.C. Wallace noted the recurring patterns in the origins and growth of "revitalization movements," beginning with the period of cultural and psychological stresses (often caused by experiences of subjugation and exploitation), followed by special psychic experiences of one or more "prophets" who become charismatic leaders with a program for constructing a new and more satisfying sociocultural system. Wallace's prime example is that of the Handsome Lake religious movement among the Iroquois at the turn of the nineteenth century. In 1799 a Seneca chief, Handsome Lake, "who had fallen upon evil days and become a drunkard," experienced visions of heavenly messengers with instructions for a new religion. The supernatural couriers announced that Handsome Lake and his people were doomed to destruction unless they completely reformed: "They must cease drinking, quarrelling, and witchcraft, and henceforth lead pure and upright lives."[12]

In a series of visions Handsome Lake received further instructions on farming and making a living, proper patterns of kinship and family relations, and so on. The movement was successful in bringing new hope and vitality to the Iroquois communities of upstate New York, and parts of this new religion have persisted to this day. As Wallace and others have pointed out, the same sequences of revitalization are visible in the origins of Christianity, as well as in the various denominations and sects of Protestantism.

Revitalization movements take many forms. Some are almost entirely religious and "otherworldly,"; others may be determinedly secular. They also differ in the extent to which they seek changes in the whole society (e.g., through revolution) versus the focus on individual self-reform. Recent studies have also detailed the ways in which ethnic movements (Black Power, Red Power, Chicano Movement, etc.),

Indian powwows with dancing, singing, and elaborate costumes are one expression of the cultural revitalization movement now ongoing among American Indians.

the Environmentalist Movement, and Health Food Movement all include some of the basic organizational stages and processes of revitalization movements — whether or not they originate from supernatural visions or "messages from heaven."

The Health Food Movement, for example, appears to have the power to bring about striking changes in individuals' personal habits, not only concerning food but also other health-related habits. Kandel and Pelto have demonstrated in their research that the Health Food Movement can be considered an alternative health care system among its adherents, although it does not necessarily replace recourse to doctors, hospitals, and other "mainline" medical resources.[14] The Health Food Movement arose in the 1960s during a time when people were experiencing greatly increased stress and anxiety concerning both the structure of society *and* personal health and well-being. For some, the Movement answers the anxieties about personal health as related to spiritual well-being, frequently in terms of religious concepts from Eastern philosophies. The various recent movements of personal salvation — including the Hari Krishna, Maharaj Ji, Reverend Moon, and others — apparently reflect increased psychological and social tensions in large segments of contemporary society. Anthropological studies of revitalization movements do not generally focus on the question of which movement is "right" or "better" than the other, but rather on the organizational processes and mechanisms that are developed among the more successful and less successful movements.

The study of human cognitive processes, the ways in which different people process and categorize information, has advanced dramatically since the early seventies. One of the fascinating developments that has sharply modified our theoretical perspectives on human cognition is the demonstration that chimpanzees are capable of using complex symbolic systems; in other words, chimpanzees have the capacity for using language. The chimpanzee Washoe, for example, is able to use aspects of the American sign language for the deaf;[15] another chimpanzee has shown the same dramatic abilities using 130 plastic symbols; and the now-famous Lana communicates effectively by means of a computer. She can read and write 71 different cards.[16]

Previously we humans believed that we are unique and alone in the ability to process symbolic information — that we alone have the brains for language and culture. The recent discoveries concerning cognitive capacities of the chimpanzees provide new foundations for understanding the evolution of human language capability.

Medical Anthropology: A New Growth Area

Medical anthropology is one of the fastest growing special subareas in anthropology. The Society for Medical Anthropology, founded in the 1960s, has grown to a membership of over 2000, including both social/cultural and physical anthropologists, as well as doctors, nurses, and other professionals interested in the intersection of social science and biomedical concerns. In earlier decades medical anthroplogy seemed to be primarily the study of the varieties of esoteric folk beliefs and traditional practices. The newer directions of research and applied activity are focused on epidemiological problems in relation to human evolution, and also on the intermingling of traditional and "modern" health care systems in contemporary urban and rural settings.

J. Laurence Angel has carried out a long-term study of the health and paleodemography of the eastern Mediterranean, primarily through intensive study of a large number of skeletal remains.[17] His analysis focuses on materials from Greece and neighboring areas, with a time span from the pre-agricultural period down to modern times. The data show, for example, that average adult longevity 30,000 years ago was approximately 33 years for males, 29 years for females. Gradually human lifespans increased in the eastern Mediterranean, reaching a high during the Classic Age of Greece, at which time adult longevity attained an average of 45 years for males, 36 for females. After the Greek "Golden Age," this measure of health and well-being declined. Not until the twentieth century did the health and nutrition conditions (and the lifespans) around the Greek Isles attain the levels they had touched in 650 B.C.!

Angel has found that long-term changes in disease patterns in the eastern Mediterranean, as in many other areas, involved increases in malaria brought about in part by clearing of lands for agriculture and by the growth of settled population clusters. Interacting with malarial infection were the hereditary blood diseases such as thalassemia and sickle-cell anemia, both of which confer some immunity *against* malaria in people who are heterozygous (one normal gene, one defective gene) even though the small minority of individuals who are homozygous (both genes defective) suffer the fatal disease. Angel has found evidence of these hereditary blood diseases in the skeletal materials, for both thalassemia and sickle-cell anemia cause enlargement of marrow space in the long bones and also porotic hyperostosis of the skull (abnormal bone growth with pitting).[18]

Haymaking is essential to support the dairy industry of Finland, the traditional base of the food production system. While rich in protein and calories, the Finnish diet is also rich in fats, including cholesterol. Nutritionists, anthropologists, and medical researchers are studying the relationships of this food pattern to the extremely high rate of heart disease in Finland.

Paleopathologists like Angel and his associates have devised improved techniques for estimating age at death, identifying probable malnutrition (from stature, bone conformations, dental problems, and other clues), and sorting out the specific disease traces affecting bone structures. A number of recent studies by paleopathologists have produced evidence that the shift from hunting and gathering toward food production, accompanied by increased populations, often meant *decline* in health and nutrition, rather than greater stability of food and well-being.

Throughout most of the world there is now active interaction between modern, university-derived medical science and the varieties of traditional healing systems. Medical anthropologists are particularly interested in the ways that people pick and choose between "modern" and "traditional" practitioners when they need medical attention. Clyde Woods and his colleagues[19] found that the people in a Guatemalan town were quite pragmatic in choosing medical alternatives. If traditional healers were unsuccessful they turned to the doctor or pharmacist, and vice versa. Difficult health problems sometimes meant a complex shuffling back and forth between the modern, the traditional, and the "intermediate" healing specialists.

Vivian Garrison has conducted extensive research[20] among Spanish-speaking people in New York, especially focusing on the use of *Espiritismo* (Spiritism) and *Santería* (Saintism) as resources for health, especially mental health, problems. *Espiritismo* is identified with Puerto Rican health practices and is derived in part from the nineteenth-century teachings of the French mystic Allen Kardec. *Santería,* on the other hand, shows much more influence from West African traditional religious and healing ideas and is especially prevalent in Cuban communities. Both these healing systems show strong influences of Catholicism, and both healing systems include trance and possession behavior by the "mediums" who practice the healing arts. *Espiritistas,* Garrison and other researchers have found, treat peoples' psychological and family problems and occasionally treat physical symptoms that are unresponsive to medical treatment. The *Espiritistas* frequently refer people to physicians for treatment of the material causes of illness, at the same time pointing out the need for the spiritual help that comes from their "working of the *causas*" — negotiating with the spirits that are bringing the patient psychic troubles and illnesses.

From Garrison's data it appears that the modes of treatment of the *Espiritistas* overlap a good deal with the services of mental health professionals, but the *Espiritistas* are more attuned to the special cultural ideas and needs of their Spanish-speaking clientele.

While some medical anthropologists have concentrated on the special health beliefs and practices of cultural groups, others have focused on particular illnesses and the sociocultural factors contributing to, or combating, the prevalence of that disease. For example, there is now a growing anthropological literature on hypertension. William Dressler[21] examined a series of social and cultural factors affecting blood pressure of people in St. Lucia in the Caribbean. He found that a major predictor of high blood pressure was *lack of social support network.* That is, individuals were under greater risk of having high blood pressure if they did not have the social support of brothers and sisters, mates and/or spouses, or other kin.

These examples are only a small part of the wide-ranging work of medical anthropologists. Often these applied researchers work closely with psychiatrists, public health officials, and various groups in medical schools, hospitals, and other

Some medical anthropologists have recently turned their attention from health problems of our urban slums to the special problems of migrant farm laborers. Following the seasonal ripening of crops, migrants move widely across the face of our continent. In the summers they are as far north as Wisconsin and Minnesota—even Canada. Winters find them gathering crops in Florida, California, and south Texas. Many of them are Spanish speaking. Their health problems stem from the fact that they are often denied access to medical facilities because they lack money and are "nonresidents" in most areas in which they travel.

These lettuce pickers in California work long hours in the hot sun for low wages. Their health problems are compounded by the new chemical pesticides and herbicides used in modern agribusiness.

health facilities. There has also been an increase in the number of anthropologists who work directly for community groups as they seek improved health services for economically and medically underserved people.

Summary

Anthropology is rather young among established academic studies and cannot claim to have produced extensive and elaborate laws or generalizations about human behavior analogous to the laws and principles of, for example, chemistry, astronomy, or physics. Much of the hundred years or so of anthropological study has been devoted to the very important task of accumulating information—the raw material about the human past and human customs and characteristics from which a mature theoretical system can be constructed.

The achievements of anthropology in the collection of descriptive materials have been considerable. Most apparent to the modern educated world is the great mass of information we now have for reconstruction of "what happened in history," the main outlines of human biological and cultural evolution from simple beginnings about three million years ago. Both human fossil materials and archaeological data supply us with the information for this aspect of anthropological interest.

Ethnographic collections about the great variety of human behavior and customs throughout the world represent another notable achievement of this first descriptive phase of the study of anthropology. Any generalizations about economic systems, religious beliefs, and "human nature," can now be built on the foundations of wide-ranging ethnographic information on hundreds of different societies.

Theoretical developments in anthropology are now beginning to emerge, developed from the accumulated descriptive ethnographies. Refinements in research on cultural evolution have been developed, and a major theoretical structure for understanding the functional organization of human behavior systems is emerging from study of the interrelations of belief systems with elements of social organization and economic arrangements. Many of the important contributions to this growing theoretical system depend on the application of psychological concepts and other theoretical ideas borrowed from related social sciences.

Notes

1. Robert J. Braidwood, "The Agricultural Revolution," *Scientific American* 203, no. 3 (1960): 130-52.

2. Marshall Sahlins, "Notes on the Original Affluent Society," in *Man the Hunter, ed. Richard Lee and Irven Devore (Chicago: Aldine, 1968):, pp. 85-89.*

3. Richard S. MacNeish, *"Ancient Mesoamerican Civilization," Science* 143 (1964): 531-37.

4. James Mellaart, Çatal Hüyük: *A Neolithic Town in Anatolia.* (London: Thames and Hudson, 1967).

5. Julian Steward, *Theory of Culture Change* (Urbana: University of Illinois Press, 1955).

6. Robert Carneiro, "A Theory of the Origin of the State, *Science* 169 (1970): 733-38.

7. John W. Bennett, *Northern Plainsmen* (Chicago: Aldine, 1969), p. 290.

8. Ibid., p. 319.

9. Andrew P. Vayda, *War in Ecological Perspective* (New York: Plenum, 1976), p. 48.

10. Bronislaw Malinowski, *Magic, Science, and Religion* (New York: The Free Press of Glencoe, 1948).

11. S. F. Nadel, "Witchcraft in Four African Societies." *American Anthropologist* 54 (1952): 18-29.

12. A.F.C. Wallace, *Religion: An Anthropological View* (New York: Random House, 1966), pp. 31-32.

13. Luther P. Gerlach and Virginia H. Hine, *People, Power, Change: Movements of Social Transformation* (Indianapolis: Bobbs-Merrill, 1970).

14. Randy F. Kandel and Gretel H. Pelto, "The Health Food Movement: Social Revitalization or Alternative Health Maintenance System," in *Nutritional Anthropology,* ed. Norge W. Jerome et al (Pleasantville, N.Y.: Redgrave, 1979).

15. Robert A. Gardner and Beatrice Gardner, "Teaching sign Language to a Chimpanzee," *Science* 165 (1969): 664-72.

16. David Rumbaugh, T. Gill, and E. von Glasensfeld, "Reading and Sentence Completion by a Chimpanzee (Pan)," *Science* 182 (1973): 731-33.

17. J. Laurence Angel, "Paleoecology, Paleodemography and Health," in Steven Polgar, editor *Population, Ecology, and Social Evolution,* ed. Steven Polgar (The Hague: Mouton, 1975), pp. 167-90.

18. Ibid.

19. Clyde Woods and Theodore Graves, *The Process of Medical Change in a Highland Guatemalan Town* (Los Angeles: University of California, 1973).

20. Vivian Garrison, "Doctor, Espiritista or Psychiatrist?: Health-seeking Behavior in a Puerto Rican Neighborhood of New York City," *Medical Anthropology* 1, no, 2 (1977): 65-188.

21. William W. Dressler, "Disorganization, Adaptation and Arterial Blood Pressure," *Medical Anthropology* 3, no. 2 (1979): 225-48.

Recommended Reading

Pfeiffer, John E. *The Emergence of Society* (New York: McGraw-Hill, 1977).

Written for the nonprofessional audience, *Emergence of Society* (subtitled: "a prehistory of the Establishment") presents an exciting panorama of human cultural and biological evolution, incorporating much data from all branches of recent anthropological research. Pfeiffer weaves an interesting tapestry of human history, with special attention to the ways in which developments in agriculture and other technology have related to growth of social institutions.

Harris, Marvin. *Cows, Pigs, Wars and Witches: The Riddle of Culture* (New York: Random House, 1974).

Very interesting controversies have continued in response to Marvin Harris's "solutions to the perplexing question of why people behave the way they do." Writing from a materialist, ecological perspective, he focuses particularly on analysis of the "sacred cow" prohibitions against beef eating in India, and the widespread Jewish-and-Islamic taboos on eating of pork. His ecological-rational explanations of widespread witch-mania in post-medieval Europe are especially fascinating reading.

Douglas, Mary. *Purity and Danger* (London: Routledge & Kegan Paul, 1966) (also Pelican and Penguin editions).

Sharply contrasting with Harris's materialist ecological explanations, the symbolic analysis of Mary Douglas seeks to explain pork prohibitions and other cultural patterns on the basis of ideational-psychological factors. The two modes of cultural analysis illustrate the wide range of theory now current in anthropological scholarship.

Sanches, Mary and Ben G. Blount. *Sociocultural Dimensions of Language Use* (New York: Academic Press, 1975).

"Children's insults: America and Samoa" is one of the 14 case studies in this collection illustrating cultural differences in communication and language use. Some of the linguistic methods used in this research are so detailed and painstaking that only dedicated professionals can follow the procedures, but the textual products are exciting works of art.

five

Fundamental Insights from Anthropological Research

Many hundreds of thousands of years ago a "human-ape" sort of creature developed innovations in brain structure and other characteristics that made possible a language-and-speech system, symbolic manipulation of ideas, and greatly increased information storage. Thus the special animal *Homo sapiens* came into being. Through a very gradual evolutionary process, we humans had become increasingly different from the great apes in physical build, as well as in the ways in which we adapt creatively to our environments by means of technology and complex sociocultural systems. In this chapter some of the fundamental insights about the human animal, derived from anthropological research and theory, will be examined.

The Concept of Culture

Culture is the word we use to label the "something that was added" that accounts for the large differences in behavior distinguishing humans from all the other animals. Culture often means simply the "social heritage" of a given group of people. The social heritage is not a "thing" that is handed down intact, like a hope chest, from generation to generation. Rather it is the complex abstraction we could build if it were possible to put together the ideas, patterns of meaning, and "rules" for behavior of all the individuals in a given community. Each new generation reshuffles and changes the systems of ideas, meanings, and rules, so that the social tradition is never fixed and unchanging in any society. Most anthropologists would agree that recognition of

70

the nature and importance of culture is the single most important insight that has marked the development of our study of humankind.

In studying and comparing cultures, we have found that practically all the important differences among the lifeways of Americans, Chinese, Australian aborigines, Inuit Pygmies of the Congo, and other peoples are understandable as *differences in learned patterns of social behavior*—not differences in biological apparatus, type of brain, type of blood, or other genetically inherited mechanisms.

The concept of culture has, of course, become commonly accepted among educated people today, so that it is difficult to realize that only fifty or sixty years ago many scholars still believed the notion that the differences in behavior of Europeans represented different biologically inherited characteristics of the "German race," the "French race," the "English race," and so forth. Recent studies and recent history have demonstrated that people are extremely versatile in adapting to large changes in cultural and social situations.

The crossing of cultural boundaries is so commonplace today that it is increasingly difficult to find people and communities that have *not* experienced profound cultural transformations in recent decades. Thousands of European, American, and Japanese people have settled in Brazil, Peru, Chile, and other Latin American countries. Workers and their families who were brought from India to the Caribbean to work on the sugar cane plantations and in other industries have adjusted readily to the cultural scenes of the West Indies. Basque peasants are sought after as sheepherders in the Western states and jai alai players in the *frontons* of Florida and Connecticut. And hundreds of sons and daughters of "stone age" New Guinea peoples now attend the University of Papua and other centers of learning. Many middle-class Americans, long accustomed to the conveniences of suburbia, have adapted quickly to the "frontier discipline" of work and simplicity in newly established rural communes.

Not quite so visible, but no less dramatic, are the radical changes in cultural beliefs and behavior that people undergo in conversion to new religious movements. In some cases religious conversions may require complete revision of food habits (e.g., to vegetarianism), rejection of alcohol and tobacco, perhaps even coffee and tea, rejection of most public recreation modes including movies, TV, and spectator sports, and—most important of all—such changes often have led to complete revamping of friendship networks and social support groups.

The dramatic, and not so dramatic, changes of cultural patterns so characteristic in today's world are striking demonstrations of the adaptability and resilience of the human behavioral system. Clearly much of human behavior is based on socially learned patterns—culture—rather than on biologically inherited "racial" characteristics.

We humans are not absolutely unique in our capacity for symbolic processes and cultural behavior. As mentioned earlier, the recent demonstrations of intellectual complexity of chimpanzees, in addition to observations of chimpanzee, gorilla, and orangutan social behavior in their wild habitats, point to the ways in which our nearest animal cousins also have *some* of these intellectual capabilities. We are not the only animal with symbolic, cultural capacity, but our recent cultural evolution has produced a human-made world of technological and social complexity far beyond the capacities of the other social animals. Some people would say that we have created an artificial cultural world beyond our own control capabilities!

Postulates of Anthropology

Our understanding of the general history of science has reached a point where we are well aware that today's accepted fundamental principles are often found tomorrow to be quaint misconceptions based on immature scholarship. Therefore, the postulates that follow should be looked at critically, with a readiness to discard any or all of them when they have outlived their usefulness. At present, these statements appear to be supported by much available evidence, and they seem to be helpful guides for research and study in anthropology and related subjects.

Culture is a total lifeway, not just a superficial set of customs. It largely shapes how we feel, behave, and perceive as we adapt to our world.   Some earlier scholars took the view that the "customs" of various people are simply a random collection of peculiar beliefs and quaint practices that are a sort of overlay, a more or less colorful glaze, on the outer surface of "natural man." Now we realize that our social heritage strongly influences how we perceive and categorize all experiences. Even our biological functioning is much shaped by culture. We get hungry at certain times of the day (in different cultures it occurs at different times) because our cultural learning has trained our physiological processes to react at regular "mealtimes." Our perceptions of sounds, colors, and other "natural" phenomena are conditioned by social experience. Many of the peoples of the world (e.g., the Navajo of the Southwest) do not distinguish between green and blue in their language, apparently because their environments make such distinctions relatively insignificant. On the other hand, Americans lump under the single word *snow* everything from slush to "dry-powdery" in a range of travel conditions that must be carefully distinguished by separate words among the Inuit, whose lives are greatly influenced by differences in kinds of snow.

Perhaps even more striking is our growing realization that illness is culturally defined and in many ways strongly influenced by cultural patterns. Psychosomatic ailments of all kinds illustrate for us the close interrelations among thoughts, beliefs, and bodily processes. Research in mental health has demonstrated great cultural differences within American society in the interpretation of psychological conditions. In different segments of the American population the same, or nearly the same, pattern of behavioral characteristics is interpreted in such phrases as "he's psycho-neurotic," "he's just acting contrary," "the devil is tempting him," "he is evil," and many other variations.

Culture can kill! And how different are the situations in various societies that can bring a person to commit suicide. In some societies the jilted lover is the most likely candidate to take his or her own life; in others it is the recipient of strong criticism from one's father. In some societies suicide is so rare that the possible motivations for such an act are hardly understood.

Cases of "voodoo death" (death by black magic) from various parts of the world provide us with another striking example of the power of cultural belief. It appears that the victim of black magic experiences profound psychophysiological shock upon learning that he or she has been "attacked" by a sorcerer. The individual loses appetite for food and water; blood pressure is reduced, blood plasma escapes into the tissues, and the heart deteriorates. He or she dies of shock that is physiologically the same as "wound shock" in war and highway casualties.

We often think of groups such as modern street gangs as being "without culture." Research has demonstrated that they often have very clearly prescribed cultural "codes" and "norms" in their rituals, membership, and territorial behavior. The territoriality of urban street gangs is often given visual display. "Trespassing" in a rival gang's domain is asking for trouble.

Every cultural system is an interconnected series of ideas and patterns for behavior in which changes in one aspect generally lead to changes in other segments of the system. We now have much evidence that in every society the techniques and actions involved in food-getting are closely related to the social organization of the society. For example, most societies in which there is heavy reliance on animal husbandry tend to emphasize the dominance of males and patrilocal choice of residence on marriage. The ethnographic evidence suggests that foraging (hunting and gathering) societies tend to have more lenient child-rearing practices than do agricultural and pastoral peoples. We have noted in the previous chapter how the areas of religious and magical belief appear to be linked to other aspects of social organization.

Studies of changes introduced into nonmodern societies have demonstrated that it is practically impossible to introduce even the simplest technological innovations without affecting other areas of culture as well. A study of the introduction by missionaries and traders of steel axes into a stone-ax-using Australian society showed that far-reaching social changes resulted from this supposedly simple technogical change.[1] The stone axes of the traditional culture had been very important, scarce status symbols, owned and controlled by the old men of high prestige and power. The new steel axes upset the entire power system by putting efficient, high-status goods in the hands of women and young men, who had previously occupied subservient positions in the society.

The introduction of a single mechanical device, the gasoline-driven snowmobile, has had far-reaching impact on cultural patterns, social organization, and the economic system of Lapland reindeer herders and North American Arctic peoples.[2]

Even games and pastimes, which are often assumed to be trivial, secondary items of behavior, are linked to particular types of social systems. Research indicates that practically none of the simpler societies have developed games of strategy. Apparently, societies must have a certain minimum of hierarchical social complexity before problems of strategy become fascinating and entertaining to individuals. Hunting and gathering peoples seem to be more attracted to games that capitalize on physical prowess.[3]

Every human cultural system is logical and coherent in its own terms, given the basic assumptions and knowledge available to the given community.   This is mainly a restatement and summary of some points that have already been made, but it deserves repeating in order to lay to rest some earlier ideas that assigned to non-European peoples a "prelogical" or childlike failure to draw appropriate conclusions from experience.

Anthropological field-workers have been unable to find any peoples in our world whose systems of reasoning or learning from experience could be called "illogical." The differences in thinking between "primitives" and "moderns" appear to lie in their fundamental assumptions about the world and things in it, conditioned by differences in available information. Modern individuals "know" that the earth revolves around the sun, rather than *vice versa*, because of the instruments of observation and calculation that have enabled a very few people in Western civilization to derive a fairly believable theory concerning the solar system. Most nonliterate peoples are in the position of relying on their eyes alone, according to which it is perfectly reasonable to regard the sun as the moving element, circling the stationary, possibly flat, earth.

Explanation of disease is another familiar area in which "modern people" have come to have some advantages over non-European thinkers. Most of us have never seen a germ. With no "objective" evidence pointing to the physical entities (germs) that have direct causal relationship to illness, nonmodern people have generally relied on the basic assumption about the universe: the world is full of supernatural spirits and powers that often cause trouble, including illness. If one grants this first premise, it then follows that illness should be treated by means of praying to, cajoling, placating, or driving out the offending supernaturals. Primitive medical practices therefore make logical sense, granted the fundamental premises. Since most people recover from illness regardless of how they are treated, folk healers and their clientele have generally had "objective evidence" testifying to the effectiveness of their curing methods.

The "snowmobile revolution" in Lapland is an interesting example of rapid socioeconomic change, stemming from a new technological development. (top) Reindeer sleds were the traditional means of transportation until the 1960s. (bottom) Sami (Lapp) reindeer herders at the gas pump. Now they, too, face the prospects of high fuel costs to maintain their economic system and new life-style.

Concerning mental illness, primitive medicine is even more interesting, for in that area the non-Western practitioner has apparently enjoyed considerable success, and non-Western concepts of therapy have in many areas anticipated modern psychiatric theory. The Iroquois Indians, for example, had in earlier times a winter ceremony in which people with obsessive dreams and other psychological problems were permitted to act out their compulsions, after their dreams had been interpreted for them by tribal "psychoanalysts."[4] It is instructive to note that primitive healers appear to have had, and in some areas still have, therapeutic effectiveness with mental illness that compares favorably with that of modern psychiatry. Such therapeutic effectiveness is not, of course, proof of the correctness of the theories of either group.

Concerning the logic of the "civilized" versus that of the "primitive," Leopold Pospisil quotes a Papuan native in a "stone age" society that was still mainly unaffected by Western culture at the time of his fieldwork in 1955.

> How can you think (asked the native) that a man can sin and can have a free will, and at the same time believe that your God is omnipotent, and that he created the world and determined all the happenings? If he determined all that happens, and (therefore) also the bad deeds, how can a man be held responsible? Why, if he is omnipotent, did the Creator have to change himself into a man and allow himself to be killed (crucified) when it would have been enough for him just to order men to behave?[5]

The man added that the Christian notion of God resembling humans in appearance seemed to him utterly "stupid."

Members of Western society have tended to consider "rationality" in terms of economic self-interest. One branch of Western thinking, economics, has built up an hypothesis of "economic man" as the basis for analysis of important social processes, and many theoreticians have come to think of "economic man" as the model for judgment of human rationality.

It seems that the assumption of "economic man" works relatively well for predicting some very gross trends in our own large-scale economy, but it does not appear wholly realistic as a yardstick in analysis of many situations in American society. For example, according to assumptions about economic rationality, working people leave areas of unemployment to move to areas of better employment possibilities. Why, then, do not all the economically deprived people of the Appalachian region leave for areas of better employment possibilities? Again, during periods when there is a relatively saturated labor market in some urban centers of the United States, why do people from some rural areas continue to migrate to these urban centers, where they will have great difficulty in finding employment?

People in modern industrialized societies, like their counterparts in peasant and tribal communities, decide on actions in terms of a great array of economic and noneconomic motives, including emotional attachments to home and community or fear and suspicion of unknown places. The economic behaviors of non-Western peoples, too, are based on seeking economic and social advantage, as well as a variety of other motives such as loyalty to kin, emotional attachment to home area and community, anxieties about the behaviors and expectations of supernatural entities (both their own and the new supernaturals of the Europeans), and many other concerns.

The behaviors and beliefs of people are often more understandable when we examine them in relation to their social networks of kin and non-kin, and in relation to the particular ecological contexts affecting their behaviors.   The example mentioned earlier in the text of the ritual pig-feasts of the Tsembaga peoples illustrates the point. The ritual killing of large numbers of pigs has social significance in cementing alliances among neighboring groups, and the periodic slaughter of animals appears to coincide with the maximum limits of pig herds in relation to available food supplies. Also, according to Rappaport, pig meat is ritually provided to the sick and to warriors thus providing high protein food at a time when people most need it.

Understanding the cultural behaviors and beliefs of peoples, and changes in their cultural patterns, is often best achieved by examining the systematic interrelationships of cultural, psychological, and ecological factors.   In chapter 4 we noted that beliefs and behaviors about witchcraft and sorcery are understandable in part through analysis of the anxieties and tensions between types of individuals in a social system. Often the areas of tensions are related to the distributions of scarce resources in the local ecological system.

Analysis of the implications, meaning, and "functions" of cultural behaviors should take into account the explicit beliefs and intentions of the people involved, but analysis must also be made of the unnoticed, unintended, other consequences (sometimes called "latent functions") of particular acts and beliefs.   One illuminating example of this principle is the custom of binding infants in cradleboards as practiced by peoples of the coastal area of British Columbia.[6] Some groups explained the custom as a beauty measure. It flattened the back of the skulls of infants in a way that was considered handsome. When the custom fell into disuse, an important unnoticed latent function of cradleboards was discovered. The cradleboard is a simple baby-tending device! When infants of crawling age were no longer kept in cradleboards, their mothers found themselves with the new task of watching to see that the baby did not crawl into the fire or fall into the nearby water. The Indian mothers did not go back to using cradleboards (partly because they are considered "primitive" by whites), but new patterns of childtending had to be developed.

Study of practically any behaviors and beliefs among nonmodern peoples, no matter how unusual, is of direct relevance to understanding our own culture, for it appears that humans everywhere shape their beliefs and behavior in response to the same fundamental human problems.   All humans everywhere seek to eat and drink enough, to get shelter from danger and physical discomfort, to secure favorable reactions from their peers, to be comforted when sick, threatened, or anxious, and to find satisfying explanations for phenomena in the observed world. The solutions to these human problems are of enormous variety, but they all give us clues to the nature of humans as cultural animals.

Human cultural behavior is extremely flexible, so that people have often developed quite different solutions to essentially similar problems. This is a reason why cultures have not all developed through identical, fixed stages of evolution, as some of the nineteenth-century evolutionists believed. But there is much evidence for the psychic and cultural oneness of humankind!

1. Striking parallels are found in cultural sequences independently developed in the early civilizations of the Old and the New World.

2. There are a large number of cultural "universals," such as language, kinship systems, modesty concerning natural functions, regulation of sexual behavior, naming of individuals, belief in a supernatural world, music and other arts, and dozens of other cultural patterns.
3. The cross-cultural statistical studies show correlations among human cultural traits that appear to be based on psychic and cultural unity.
4. Anthropologists have found no people whose system of language and logic was incomprehensible.

Many traditional cultural practices and beliefs that once seemed quaint and outmoded have found to have a pragmatic basis.   Perhaps the most telling example of "folk wisdom" is in the dozens of medicinal herbs that were the inventory of North American Indian healing methods before the coming of the Europeans. For example, Bernard Ortiz de Montellano has reported on the pharmacological examination of some Aztec medicinal herbs in relation to what the Aztec physicians believed about them. He found, "of the 25 plants dealt with...16 would produce most of the effects claimed in native sources, 4 may possibly be active, and 5 do not seem to possess the activity claimed by native informants."[7] Dozens, even hundreds, of medicinal herbs from the folklore of Europe, Africa, and the American Indians, have been found to be useful for salves, emetics, cathartics, analgesics, and other medical uses.

In a similar vein the "old wives' tale" that breast-feeding suppresses ovulation, and hence contributed to birth spacing, has been found to have a scientific basis—in some populations under particular nutritional conditions.

Individuals, even in small-scale traditional societies, differ one from another in attitudes, information, skills, culturally valued resources, and other attributes.   The image of nonmodern peoples as "all alike," bound to a single, homogeneous cultural tradition, is a misleading one, based on superficial and careless observation.

Researchers in the "six cultures" study, mentioned earlier, found that child-training practices of parents differed more intraculturally than they did across cultures. In a similar vein, R. Pollnac found broad variations among Baganda people of Uganda in their categorizing of plants, sorting of color terms, and other cognitive patterns.[8]

The study of intracultural variations in behavior and beliefs throws new light on the ways that cultural influences, environmental factors, and individual characteristics intersect. Ralph Bolton, for example, studies variations in individual aggressiveness of men in a highland Andean community and identified differences in blood sugar levels that he believed accounted, at least in part, for the observed differences in aggressiveness.[9]

B. R. DeWalt studied the different adaptive strategies of Mexican peasants in a village undergoing rapid change in connection with largescale agricultural development programs. He found at least three different adaptive patterns within the seemingly homogeneous community: some individuals were specializing in livestock, some in growing feed crops, and still others focused their farming efforts on the traditional maize. The economically most successful individuals were able to com-

The study of aggressive behavior is an example of a multidisciplinary problem that involves research by various social scientists. These little girls in an inner-city neighborhood illustrate the fact that our stereotypes about male and female roles are not always accurate.

bine two or three of these into a "mixed portfolio" of economic investments.[10] Other recent studies have demonstrated the significance of intracultural differences in kinship designations, personality styles, adoption of modern medical practices, use of alcohol, and a variety of other attributes.

Explanation of human behavior is essentially one-sided and incomplete unless information about our biological, cultural, social, and psychological characteristics is taken into account, together with information about our biophysical environment. This fundamental insight provides the rationale for the holistic, integrating style of research that characterizes the study of anthropology.

From the biological side of anthropological studies, these further insights must be added.

Although the peoples of the world may be roughly (and arbitrarily) categorized into major population groups, based on a very limited number of physical characteristics, there are no "pure races" and there never have been. Many population groups are "intermediate" in skin color and other characteristics, so that no sharp "boundaries" can be identified to separate "Negroid," "Caucasoid," and "Mongoloid" peoples. (Many anthropologists have dropped the use of the term *race* altogether as a label denoting different kinds of populations.)

There is no evidence of significant differences in ability or "intelligence" among the major ethnic or "racial" groupings of the world. Contrary to the claims of A.

Jensen and others, the results of IQ tests, as given in our schools, do not demonstrate hereditary differences in mental abilities among population groups.

1. No IQ tests have been developed that can measure the purely hereditary, "culture-free" capabilities of individuals.
2. No satisfactory means have been demonstrated for statistically sorting out the "nature" from the "nurture" factors in IQ tests. In addition, the *situational factors* in testing cannot be satisfactorily standardized, given the significant differences in the symbolic meaning of the school environment for different ethnic groups.

Anthropologists (and other scientists) have discovered no human biological characteristics that are unaffected by life experiences and environmental conditions. Conversely, no human characteristics of thought or action can be regarded as unaffected by genetically inherited biological factors. Anthropologists have frequently clashed with advocates of "white supremacy," "Aryan superiority," and other forms of racism. Such racists, from Count Gobineau a century ago down to Adolph Hitler and some contemporary white "chauvinists," have either ignored the anthropological evidence altogether or else grossly distorted those materials for their own prejudiced purposes. The central premise of anthropologists in opposition to the racists continues to be *practically all the significant differences in behavior among human populations (including expression of attitudes, "intelligence," and other psychological characteristics) are understandable as ecologically influenced, learned cultural patterns, rather than biologically inherited characteristics.*

Major Problems for Research

Our inventory of the research achievements in anthropology actually represents only a bare initial framework for a science of human behavior. Each of the postulates listed above raises dozens of pertinent research questions. Detailed, precise knowledge that would effectively predict human cultural behavior under particular circumstances is still very far from realization. Anthropologists need more precise tools for observing, recording, and analyzing human biocultural evolution and behavior.

Methodological Problems

Anthropological observation must be developed to adequately reflect the great variations in behavior found in even the simplest societies. Until recent times anthropologists have paid little attention to problems of "adequate samples" and representativeness of their data. It had been felt that the behavior of nonliterate peoples is so bound by custom that there is little variation, so that deviations from custom are readily recognizable.

Anthropological fieldwork must eliminate or at least minimize the effects of the emotional biases of the observer. (One way of partially achieving this goal is through team research, in which several observers with different points of view carry out fieldwork in the same community.)

Standard units of observation or behavior that are equally applicable in a wide range of different cultures should be devised. Many of our earlier categories of observation (e.g., patrilocal residence, fertility rites, polytheism, hunting-and-gathering society) are rough-and-ready pigeonholes into which we place a rather mixed bag of actual behavior. More refined concepts are needed in practically all aspects of human behavior.

Theoretical constructs such as "acculturation," "individualism," "social disorganization," "cultural disorganization," "cooperation," "male dominance," and many others need more refined *operational* definitions.

Anthropologists, as well as other social and biological scientists, are in need of more refined and systematic ways to combine *quantified,* statistical data analysis with carefully defined *qualitative* information. Too often researchers have taken an "either-or" attitude about these two styles of data collection, instead of combining the best features of both.

Refined and carefully designed use of computerized analysis can permit anthropologists to develop complex models of human behavior in which cultural, situational, physical, economic, and other variables can be examined in systematic interaction. However, sophisticated statistical analysis requires more careful collection of field data.

There is a continued need for more multidisciplinary team research projects, combining biological data, sociocultural materials, assessment of environmental features, and other ecological data. Effective testing of the problems anthropologists are now dealing with often requires more than a single, "lone wolf" field-worker.

There is a clear need for new research techniques that bridge the gap from individual small-scale communities to the larger sociopolitical systems in which they are imbedded. There is now widespread recognition of the importance of "macro-level analysis," but techniques must be devised for studying these processes at more abstracted levels, far from the face-to-face levels of human behavior.

All the suggested modifications and improvements in field research still place very heavy reliance on the time-tested methods of participant observation and informant interviewing that are the hallmarks of anthropology.

Theoretical Problems

As has been suggested above, the theoretical problems crying for research are so numerous that any listing seems pointless or distorted. However, here are some intriguing questions that have frequently haunted anthropologists.

To what extent is it possible (and likely) for societies to maintain diversity, even disagreement, on basic values and beliefs and still remain viable, "organized" social systems?   Earlier anthropological (and other social) theory laid great stress on the need for a society to have a consensus of values, or agreement on norms, in order to be healthy. More recently, there has been increasing logical and empirical evidence that such unanimity concerning major values and attitudes is not a *sine qua non* for interaction and cooperation even in simpler social systems.

To what extent is it possible (and likely) for peoples to change their beliefs and practices rapidly without suffering cultural disintegration and mental disorder?   Again, the earlier position of anthropologists has been that rapid culture change is inevitably disruptive and unhealthy. All cultures change, however, and most peoples in the world today are experiencing relatively rapid change. The great theoretical problem is how much and what kinds of changes are "disruptive" and "mentally harmful?"

To what extent can similar types of developments in cultural evolution be found among the diverse environments and cultures in the world?   This is the question which the nineteenth-century evolutionists thought they had answered and to which modern anthropologists have now returned with renewed interest.

To what extent, in terms of standards such as mental and physical health, can evaluations be made about some cultural patterns and systems being "better" or "healthier" than others?   Many anthropologists take the view that no absolute judgments can be made concerning the merits of different cultural patterns and systems. On the other hand, those in applied anthropology are engaged in numerous development programs where such cultural evaluations must be made. Billions of dollars are being spent by governments and private agencies in technical assistance, aid to "developing nations," and many other programs that are based on assumptions concerning relative "backwardness," "progress," and other value judgments. The value judgments involved in the application of these intentions to specific communities are most often left unexamined. Some of the most interesting new knowledge in applied anthropology is in the area of the "unintended consequences" of particular development projects.

Of course, the anthropologist's primary task is not evaluation of cultural patterns as "better" or "worse," for such normative judgments often lead to subjective (and faulty) ethnographic observation. The most important work in anthropology will be in the building of theory in terms of which the varieties of human behavior can become more understandable and predictable. Without such understanding, well-intentioned programs of development and "modernization" can often result in much unintended cultural disorganization and human suffering among the people who are supposed to benefit from such programs.

Summary and Conclusions

Our human abilities to create and to manipulate systems of symbolic communication mark us as distinct from other animals. The various symbol systems—the cultures—of different peoples can all be regarded as ways of adapting to particular environments. Cultural customs must be examined, therefore, in the total context of circumstances in which they occur. We have now accumulated a respectable inventory of cultural descriptions both past and present relating to different environments; an exciting new stage of anthropological study appears to be in the making.

Anthropology is often considered a collection of curious facts, telling about the peculiar appearance of exotic people and describing their strange customs and beliefs. It is looked upon as an entertaining diversion, apparently without bearing upon the conduct of life of civilized communities.

This opinion is mistaken. More than that, I hope to demonstrate that a clear understanding of the principles of anthropology illuminates the social processes of our own times and may show us, if we are ready to listen to its teaching, what to do and what to avoid.[11]

Notes

1. Lauriston Sharp, "Steel Axes for Stone Age Australians," in *Human Problems in Technological Change,* ed. Edward H. Spicer (New York: Russell Sage Foundation, 1952).

2. Pertti J. Pelto, *The Snowmobile Revolution: Technology and Social Change in the Arctic* (Menlo Park, Calif.: Cummings, 1973).

3. John M. Roberts, Malcolm J. Arth, and Robert R. Bush, "Games in Culture," *American Anthropologist,* 61 (1959): 597-605.

4. F. C. Wallace, "The Institutionalization of Cathartic and Control Strategies in Iroquois Religious Psychotherapy," in *Culture and Mental Disorder,* ed. M. K. Opler (New York: The Macmillian Co., 1959), pp. 63-96.

5. Leopold Pospisil, *The Kapauku Papuans of West New Guinea* (New York: Holt, Rinehart, and Winston, 1963), p. 85.

6. From Clellan S. Ford as cited by Ward Goodenough in *Cooperation in Change* (New York: Russell Sage Foundation, 1963), pp. 81-82.

7. Bernard Ortiz de Montellano, "Empiriical Aztec Medicine," *Science* 188 (1977): 215-20.

8. Richard Pollnac, "Intra-cultural Variability in the Structure of the Subjective Color Lexicon in Buganda," *American Ethnologist* 2(1975): 89-109.

9. Ralph Bolton, "Aggression and Hypoglycemia among the Qolla: A Study in Psychobiological Anthropology," *Ethnology* 12 (1973): 227-57.

10. Billie R. DeWalt, *Modernization in a Mexican Ejido: A study in Economic Adaptation* (New York: Cambridge University Press, 1979).

11. Franz Boas, *Anthropology and Modern Life* (New York: W.W. Norton and Co., 1928).

Recommended Reading

Wallace, A.F.C. *Rockdale: The Growth of an American Village in the Early Industrial Revolution* (New York: Knopf, 1978).

This account of the evolution of textile machinery in one small manufacturing district in Pennsylvania is a richly researched documentation of cultural processes that relates anthropological insights with the history of America's 19th century.

Bernard, H.R. and P.J. Pelto. *Technology and Social Change* (New York: Macmillan, 1972).

The growing documentation of technological change and its relationships with social and cultural systems is particularly significant in relation to current social issues involving the "energy crisis," automation, and post-industrial society. This book presents ten important cases concerning the cultural and human implications of new technology.

Landy, David. *Culture, Disease and Healing* (New York, Macmillan, 1977).

The rapidly developing interrelationships between anthropology and biomedical concerns is well-illustrated in this collection of papers that range from descriptions of folk medicine to case studies of interactions between modern and traditional health systems.

six

Suggested Methods for Teachers

Raymond H. Muessig

... There is hope, I believe, in seeing the human adventure as a whole and in the shared
trust that knowledge about mankind, sought in reverence for life, can bring life.

Margaret Mead, *Blackberry Winter*[1]

Introduction

The unitary theme articulated by Dr. Mead has also been expressed by Professor
Pelto in the first chapter of this book. Pelto writes that the anthropologist feels that the
fundamental principles of cultural and social systems can be discovered only through
studying the whole range of human behavioral patterns. Anthropology's range,
potential for integrating past and present knowledge from diverse disciplines, rich
literature, attractive content, humane quality, and seemingly endless methodological
possibilities at the elementary and secondary levels are some of its appeals. Not only
is anthropology an enriching and enjoyable field to study, but it makes a very real
contribution as an insightful, sensitive social science. And, as Morris Freilich puts it,
"Today, as perhaps never before, the world needs good social science: we need to
understand man, society, and culture, before all of these phenomena disappear in
the war that *will* end all wars."[2]

This chapter presents selected teaching strategies that have been designed to
make anthropology in particular and social studies education in general more
pleasurable, personal, diversified, inviting, stimulating, and significant. There are

84

many more possibilities for elementary and secondary classroom activities than can be included in the available space. I hope that readers and their students will feel that I have selected well among the various alternatives.

Providing Opportunities for Learners to Develop an Increasingly Meaningful Understanding of Culture

In chapter 5, Dr. Pelto observes that most anthropologists would agree that recognition of the nature and importance of culture is the single most important insight that has marked the development of our study of humankind. He stresses the importance of culture when he says that *practically all the significant differences in behavior among human populations (including expression of attitudes, "intelligence," and other psychological characteristics) are understandable as ecologically influenced, learned cultural patterns, rather than biologically inherited characteristics.*

To introduce learners from the fifth through the twelfth grades to the meaning of culture, some of its components, and its consequences, the teacher might secure from various libraries sources written at different reading levels that define and illustrate the concept of culture. Dictionaries, encyclopedias, fiction and nonfiction works related to such areas as ethnography, ethnology, archaelogy, and sociocultural anthropology could be made readily available on classroom bookshelves and/or a large table. The teacher might invite every pupil to look into some of the sources that have been gathered, to locate one to three definitions of culture, and to record the definitions on scratch paper. A stack of around seventy 5″ x 8″ lined cards and six or seven fluid markers with ink in different colors could be placed on the teacher's desk. Then, every class member might be asked to print one definition of culture per card. If a participant were to use a definition by Pelto in this book, for example, a lettered card would say

CULTURE OFTEN MEANS SIMPLY THE "SOCIAL
HERITAGE" OF A GIVEN GROUP OF PEOPLE

After all the cards have been completed and turned into the teacher, they could be displayed throughout the classroom. The teacher might then move around the room, read aloud from some of the cards to the entire class, and encourage a discussion of the printed definitions. Next, the teacher could help the class to use parts of the definitions that have been discussed to develop its own composite definitions. Boys and girls in grades five and six might devise a class definition such as this: "Culture is the way of life of a people." Seventh through ninth graders could work together in constructing a sentence that says, "Culture is the total way of life of a group of people that is passed on from one generation to another." Senior high school students might draft the following: "Culture includes all of the learned behavior transmitted from one generation to another in a given society."

As soon as learners have some grasp of the definition of culture they have composed and discussed, the teacher might move the class into a closely related approach that can broaden and deepen an understanding of culture. At this point, each participant could be provided with a supply of 3″ x 5″ cards (perhaps 10 cards in grades 5-6, 15 cards in grades 7-9, and 20 cards in grades 10-12). The teacher might get class members started by saying something similar to this:

Would each of you use his or her imagination for about the next ten minutes? Please pretend that you are a small bird. (A student in grades 9-12 might prefer to be an invisible person or to create his or her own device.) Your name is Drib. You are able to see and hear many things by flying over the ground and by perching in trees and on bushes and rocks. You are really intelligent, and you can even write by using your beak as a pen and the juice of berries as ink. Your nest is close to a small village in which children, women, and men of the Ebirt tribe live.

A good friend of yours is a rabbit whose name is Tibbar. While you two are talking one day, Tibbar says, "Say, Drib, do you happen to know anything about culture? Esuom, the mouse, used that word last week. I asked what it meant. Esuom told me but did not give me any examples of things I could look for to find out about the culture of a people. For instance, would *language* or *dress* be included in the idea of culture? Drib, you must know a lot about our Ebirt neighbors, flying from place to place in their village as you do so often. Would you please think about this matter a little bit and then make a list for me of some general things that might help someone to study the Ebirt culture—or the culture of almost any group of human beings, for that matter?"

You want to help Tibbar. You have some cards. You decide to write down one example of culture on each of the cards.

After each learner has completed his or her set of cards and turned them in, the teacher might form a committee of five students by taking the class roll and asking the last five people in alphabetical order to serve. The committee members would place all of their classmates' cards into a shoe box, find a place where the cards could be spread out (e.g., the school library or cafeteria), eliminate all duplicate examples, and give the teacher the remaining cards in no special order. Meeting with the entire class, the teacher might pick any 10-20 cards and ask questions such as the following:

Would *tools and the way they are used* be an example of the *culture* of a people? Why, or why not?

Could *housing* be a part of the *culture* of a group? Why, or why not?

Might a *lake* be an ingredient in *culture?* Why, or why not?

Do you think *food habits* should be included in *cultural* forms? What reasons could you offer, one way or the other?

How about *trees?*

Would *play* be something you might regard as a characteristic of a *culture?* Why, or why not?

Should *belief in life after death* be on our list as something to look for in the *culture* of a society? Why might you include this or leave it out?

Is *rain* a good example of *culture?* Why, or why not?

What do you want to do with *rocks?*

Questions such as these could launch an interesting, meaningful, and even controversial exchange in which a number of nuances might emerge. Learners might agree quite easily, for instance, that *music* could be used as an acceptable aspect of a given culture, but what about a *mountain?* A mountain is a *natural* elevation of the earth's surface that may well have existed a long time before a particular group of people came anywhere near it. Yet, what if the mountain becomes an important part of the beliefs of a society, the home of their god or gods, the site of some of their most sacred ceremonies? "Is the mountain then 'cultural,' or are just actions and values associated with it?" some students might ask. In any event, early and complete closure is unnecessary, and perhaps even undesirable, at this stage. The methodological recommendation that follows could sustain a spirit of tentativeness with respect to the ingredients of culture.

The teacher might ask the first five people in alphabetical order on the class list to form a new committee. This committee could be invited to assemble a list of 30-40 examples of culture so there would be at least one cultural component for each class member. The 3″ x 5″ cards just discussed by the class that contain interesting illustrations of culture and those cards remaining in the shoe box that provide appealing cultural forms would be used to compile the list. Although a student-developed list would probably reveal different conceptual levels, a certain amount of overlapping, and a few misunderstandings, most shortcomings would not present a serious problem at this stage and could even foster additional learning and sophistication. At any rate, the committee's list—anticipating some variations in grades 5-12—might look something like this:

architecture	media of exchange
ceremonies	medicines
child-rearing practices	music
dance	myths
drama	painting
drawing	pets
dress	play
enemies	prayers
folktales	religion
gestures	rites of passage
housing	sayings
humor	sculpture
institutions	social classes
jewelry	beauty standards
kinship systems	taboos
language	techniques
laws	tools
leaders	totems
legends	weapons

Next, the teacher could ask the best printer in the class to print the committee's list on large, lined sheets of experience chart paper, which would then be thumbtacked to the bulletin boards in the room. At this point, the teacher would invite each learner to choose an item on the list which he or she would like to investigate. Having selected "child-rearing practices" or "dress" or "play" or "tools" or some other item, the pupil would put his or her initials next to the example of culture. If more than one student would like to read, think, and write about the same cultural ingredient, that would be fine; and small groups could be formed.

Since the teacher is concerned primarily here with encouraging learners to under-stand and to apply some cultural components, the American society, with which the majority of class members would be most familiar, might be used for illustrative purposes the first time this teaching strategy is used. However, if a similar approach seems desirable in the future for various reasons, committees of four to six students could be formed, with each committee selecting a well-researched society in a different part of the world. In this way, what will be learned at this stage could be readily transferred and reinforced. This time, therefore, the teacher would ask everyone to look into, to reflect on, and to produce 100-200 words about an item in an American context. The teacher might stimulate inquiry by moving from individual to individual and small group to small group and asking questions such as the following at different grade levels:

> *Do you think that music is a part of the American culture? Why, or why not? If so, might you learn more about American culture by including music in your study than you would by leaving music out? Why, or why not? Do Americans have any music that came from other cultures? Why, or why not? Have people in the United States created any music of their own? Why, or why not? Have other cultures used American music? Why, or why not? (These questions could be adapted easily for various uses in grades five through twelve.)*
>
> *Should totems be listed among the properties found in the culture of the United States? What reasons can you give for and against including totems? In American professional football and baseball, are bears, eagles, lions, falcons, rams, seahawks, broncos, bengals, dolphins, colts, tigers, cubs, cardinals, orioles, and bluejays examples of totems? Why, or why not? Why would you, or wouldn't you, regard pintos, mustangs, broncos, thunderbirds, bobcats, cougars, firebirds, and other such names for American automobiles as totems? What about the American bald eagle? Is it, or isn't it, a totem in this society? Should you include American Indians, Amerindians, Native Americans, or specific tribes in your investigation and consider the snake, the wolf, the eagle, the bear, the salmon, and the like? Why, or why not? As you think about totems as a possible cultural form in the United States, are you more sure or less positive about what you should write in your short paper? Why? (Questions like these could be used with some junior high school and many senior high school students. Again, final answers are not being sought here. A search for gradual, increasing understanding is being encouraged.)*

As soon as each individual and/or small group has turned in the 100-200 words about an item in an American context, the teacher might form a third committee for editing and writing purposes, composed of the middle four people in alphabetical order from a class list. (In a class of thirty, for example, the fourteenth, fifteenth, sixteenth, and seventeenth students would be chosen.) This committee would (1) read all of the papers on examples of culture in American society, (2) correct all errors in spelling, grammar, punctuation, and syntax, with the assistance of the teacher, (3) arrange the essays in some kind of order, (4) write an introduction, headings, subheadings, transitions, and a conclusion, and (5) develop the first draft of a class booklet. (The teacher could ask at this point for volunteers who might like to prepare appropriate illustrative material to increase the appeal of the production.) The teacher would go over the initial version, make final corrections, and ask the school or district office to type and reproduce enough copies so there could be a copy for each class member, each learner's family and others (such as the principal, the appropriate elementary and/or secondary supervisor, the curriculum director, the superintendent, the members of the school board, and the district public relations person) who would like to see what has been accomplished by the class and the teacher. With the booklets to family members and others would go a letter explaining the project briefly and inviting everyone receiving the publication to a special open house one evening specified in the future.

With the open house as an incentive, class members could be receptive to the formation of two more committees. The fourth committee in this sequence of learning activities would be composed of eight people, who occupy the sixth through thirteenth alphabetical positions in a class list and who would prepare attractive, colorful bulletin boards, murals, and/or collages around the classroom that depict examples of cultural forms in the U.S. The other committee would also be made up of eight members, listed 18-25 in the teacher's roll book. From the closets, basements, attics, garages, tool sheds, barns, and so on, of relatives, friends, neighbors, and others, learners in this group would gather physical evidence, realia, illustrating and vivifying ingredients in American culture, which could be displayed in the special classroom night "museum" for visitors to see, handle, consider, and discuss. The exhibit might include such diverse things as tools, blueprints, pens, publications, coins, stamps, good luck charms, dresses, hats, work clothes, shoes, empty medicine bottles, forms of makeup, suntan aids, hair curlers, necklaces, earrings, cuff links, toys, sports equipment, sheet music, wood carvings, models, and paintings. The teacher might prepare a handout for each guest that contains (1) a paragraph reviewing the "whys" and "whats" of the series of class activities associated with examples of culture, (2) the student-developed list of suggested cultural forms, and (3) an invitation to try to match the list to the "museum collection" to see which ingredients of culture might be represented. In addition to providing positive reinforcement for the learners' efforts and achievements, the evening in the classroom might result in a learning experience for parents and others.

I had senior high school students in mind when I developed the last two suggested methods for this initial section of the chapter, but the following two ideas might be adapted for use with some learners in grades seven through nine. As a lead-in for this next approach, the teacher could read aloud to a class a passage from *The Golden Peninsula: Culture and Adaptation in Mainland Southeast Asia* by Charles F. Keyes. Professor Keyes writes:

> . . . Culture, as I understand it, is a system of meaning. Such meaning is expressed in forms that are directly observable and also invested with a content that must be elicited.
>
> Cultural forms include all types of expressive actions (such as speech, gestures, play, ritual, and music), art, written documents, architecture, as well as more mundane implements of daily life, tools, dress, and so on. In short, cultural forms are as observable as are aspects of the landscape, as the number of people living in a settlement, or as the rice placed in a granary. They are certainly more easily observable than the psychological needs that motivate people to action. Cultural forms in and of themselves have only a limited utility for the student; one must also know what content these forms carry for the people for whom they are meaningful. . . . [3]

Students who have progressed through the sequence of activities suggested up to this point should have a good grasp of the "cultural forms" to which Keyes has referred above. Hence, a class could focus at this stage on the *meaning* that elements of culture might have for a given group of people. Since the automobile is such an important component in American life, and since many students in grades ten through twelve are intensely interested in cars, the teacher's approach might utilize the automobile. As an initiatory activity, the teacher might walk briefly with a class around the high school parking lot and a few adjacent blocks in the neighborhood, just offering and soliciting casual remarks about the variety of old and new cars. (If students want to include motorcycles, recreational vehicles, vans, and pickups in a relaxed exchange about various motor vehicles, they should be encouraged to do so.) Then, back in the classroom, the teacher could invite a response to questions such as these:

In the United States, would you regard the automobile as a cultural form—or at least a part of a cultural form, such as the technology of this society? Why, or why not? If so, what could be some of the things that the automobile might mean to Americans?

Perhaps participants would answer the last question above with comments similar to the following:

I think a lot of Americans care about their freedom. Whether they know it or not, I'll bet the automobile means freedom to people. You know, freedom to go where they want to when they want to. Americans use cars to move, to see things in a lot of places, to get away from problems, and a lot of stuff. I suppose cars are big with us high school students because they're a way to avoid our parents and to be alone with each other.

A bunch of us Americans love our technology, and we're really proud of the automobile. I mean, our cars are convenient, and dependable, and fast, and quiet—well, sometimes—, and air-conditioned, and all that. We can have power brakes and steering and windows and seats and trunks. The automobile means jobs and fun and even beauty to a lot of us.

What I want to say is, I think cars mean something to us all right, like others in our class have been saying. OK? But I have a feeling that different cars mean different things to different people at different times in their lives. Does that make any sense to anybody here?

A statement such as the last one would create a beautiful opportunity for the teacher to move immediately into a refinement of the discussion that has just been taking place. The teacher might hold up, display on chalk trays, or pass around the class mounted enlargements of photographs such as those illustrated in figure 4. (I took the shots for figure 4 in about one hour one afternoon. The teacher who does not know how to photograph, process, enlarge, and mount the pictures needed for this activity should be able to get the help of a class member, a friend, a fellow teacher, the school photography club, or the director of the high school or district instructional media center.)

Figure 4.

91

Then, the teacher could say something like the following:

> *Let's all look at these photographs of eight automobiles. Is it possible that the cars pictured here might "mean different things to different people at different times in their lives?" Why, or why not?*
>
> *Now, shall we take the photos one at a time and try to imagine what the particular car might mean to its owner? How about this one? (The teacher could walk in front of every class member, holding the photograph classified as photo 4-A so it can be studied briefly by each person.)*
>
> *The teacher would guide a discussion of all the automobile photographs in this way. With respect to photo 4-F, for instance, a senior high school student could comment in this manner:*

> Well, a 'Vette like the one in the picture might mean a bunch of things to its owner. But I sort of have to make up an owner before I try to guess what the owner's feelings might be about this car. OK?
>
> The owner might be between, say, 20 to 28 years old. Right? Because it takes bread for the down payment and the big monthly payments for maybe three years or so to buy this baby. A Corvette costs too much to be a first car for most of us. And the insurance for a sports car when you're younger is humongous. A lot of owners of 'Vettes could usually be under 28, I think, because this isn't a good car for a family. I mean, it only has two seats, and it really doesn't have what you could call a "trunk." Oh, and this bus is hard on gas, too. When you've only been married a few years, with a kid or two, you can't waste a lot of bread.
>
> Then, more dudes buy 'Vettes than chicks, so I'm gonna say that this is a guy's car. It can be a tricky car to handle at high speeds on curves. There isn't much weight on the rear wheels that push it, so it can spin out on you. You should know somethin' about wheels to take care of a car like this, too. Keeping it tuned and all. Hey, and I don't mean to be sexist or anything, all right?
>
> OK, so now I'm ready to talk about what I think the car in the picture might mean to the owner I've made up. First of all, I feel this car means "mucho macho" to the dude. He thinks, "I can really make out with wheels like this. I should have to beat the chicks off of me with a club!" He believes that owning a 'Vette makes him more important, gives him instant status, you know? He likes the car's looks and the feeling of power and speed. With the T-top out, he feels free with the sun on him and the wind rushin' by during the day, and he feels romantic when he and his chick can look up and see the moon and the stars when they park at night. He thinks, "Man, this is really livin'!"

This initial section of this chapter has been devoted to providing opportunities for learners to develop an increasingly meaningful understanding of culture. This concluding activity is for senior high school students and is concerned with cultural "universals," to which Professor Pelto refers in chapter 5. He says, "There are a large number of cultural 'universals' such as language, kinship systems, modesty concerning natural functions, regulations of sexual behavior, naming of individuals, belief in a supernatural world, music and other arts, and dozens of other cultural patterns."

Using the seven examples of cultural "universals" provided by Pelto in the preceding quotation as headings for committees, the teacher could form seven groups of three to five students, depending on the size of the class. The teacher might ask the first seven people in alphabetical order on the class list to serve as chairpersons for the different committees, the second seven to function as librarians for each group, the third seven to work as designers, the fourth seven to act as scribes, and the fifth seven (in the event of a large class) to perform as arrangers. The chairpersons would facilitate the activities of their committee members, serve on a central class coordinating committee, and confer with the teacher on progress and problems. The librarians would secure relevant materials for the people in their respective committees and trade sources between and among groups. The designers would create a large wall chart in the form of a matrix, as suggested in figure 5. The scribes would enter information on the wall chart. The arrangers would place tables, desks, chairs, etc., where they are needed in the classroom and elsewhere for committee meetings, independent investigation, and so on. Everyone in the class would do his or her share of the research necessary to make the cultural "universals" activity successful and significant. Those participants who might like to trade basic assignments (librarian to designer and vice versa, for example) could do so.

Working with librarians and others in the school, the community, colleges, universities, museums, and so on, the teacher would help the class librarians to secure materials that are as interesting, readable, varied, and complete as possible on five to eight societies. In addition to books,[4] articles, booklets, encyclopedias, tapes, photograph collections, slides, filmstrips, films, realia, resource people (e.g., anthropologists or former members of the Peace Corps), and the like could also be used.

After appropriate societies have been selected, their names would be entered on the wall chart to form the vertical columns of the matrix. "Society A" in figure 5 might become "The Dusun," "Society B" could be "The Sonjo," and so on.

Let us assume that a member of Committee #6, Belief in a Supernatural World, is investigating whether this cultural "universal" seems to hold true for "The Dusun" in the first vertical column. The student could turn to *The Dusun: A North Borneo Society* by Thomas Rhys Williams. This 100-page paperback is one of the *Case Studies in Cultural Anthropology* edited by George and Louise Spindler, which include similarly brief works on societies such as the Palauan, Gopalpur, Tiwi, Swazi, Tepoztlan, Gururumba, and Igbo. In Williams' text the student would discover that Chapter 3 is introduced by the subheading "Belief in a Supernatural World," which is identical to Pelto's wording and the title of Committee #6. The student might then copy the following and give it to the committee scribe, who would record it in the appropriate rectangle on the wall chart:

> In Dusun life there are a series of personal and community-wide crises that lead to fear of the unknown. The personal crises of birth, sickness, death, individual fortune, success in hunting, yield of crops, and outcome of personal disputes are marked by Dusun as events in which it is necessary to deal with the forces responsible through engaging in specific ritual behavior. Community crises of flood, drought, epidemic disease, and war similarly are dealth with through ritual behavior.

The people of Sensuron believe there is a direct relationship between the crises of life and a world of supernatural beings and unseen forces. It is also believed generally that proper ritual actions can be interposed between men and supernatural beings and forces in attempts to modify or control events causing fear, pain, or uncertainty.[5]

Cultural "Universals"	Society A	Society B	Society C	Society D	Society E	Society F
Committee # 1 Language						
Committee # 2 Kinship Systems						
Committee # 3 Modesty Concerning Natural Functions						
Committee # 4 Regulations of Sexual Behavior						
Committee # 5 Naming of Individuals						
Committee # 6 Belief in a Supernatural World						
Committee # 7 Music and Other Arts						

Figure 5.

In the event that a committee member might not be able to locate information on a particular cultural "universal" in a given society, the scribe would write "no information" on that part of the matrix. Should it seem doubtful whether a cultural "universal," such as "music and other arts" applies in a selected society, the scribe could put "unlikely" or some such word in the correct space. If it is certain that a cultural "universal" is not present in a society, the scribe could record "does not apply" on the wall chart.

Every student should be encouraged to read all the entries on the wall chart during times reserved for independent study in the class. Then, the teacher would lead a general class discussion that could help the group summarize points that have been learned about cultural "universals" in particular and the unity and diversity of humankind in general.

Having Fun Applying the Concept of "Culture" to Other Animals

Just as people from ages 5 to 95 can learn about the concept of culture and about themselves through the study of other cultures, so also can they gain insights through an examination of the learned behavior of other creatures in the animal kingdom.

Every analogy has its limitations, of course, and the purpose of the methodological recommendations that follow is to have fun playing with some intriguing questions and to fire imaginations, not to try to arrive at anything approaching definitive answers. Learners in grades K-12 can enjoy and profit from activities relating to other animals to which the idea of culture is applied and its boundaries explored. Queries such as the following may emerge and lead elementary and secondary pupils toward greater enlightenment:

Do any other animals have a "culture" of their own which they teach their young? Why, or why not?
Can one animal learn the "culture" of another animal? Why, or why not?
Can humankind learn the "culture" of other animals? Why, or why not?
Can other animals learn the "culture" of humankind? Why, or why not?

With a few variations, progressing from concrete to appropriate, varied levels of abstraction, the initial activity proposed here can be adjusted for use at all grade levels. Although a photograph of a puppy could be used here, it would be more concrete, appealing, dramatic, and memorable to have a real, live young dog to see and to touch. (The pup might be borrowed from a friend, neighbor, person running a classified advertisement in a community weekly, kennel, or pet store.) The teacher's questioning might proceed as far as possible with a given class along these lines:

What am I holding here?
Will you please tell me as much as you can about what you see? Now, take another good look at the puppy, and then look at each other. In what ways do you and the puppy look like each other? (Both the children and the dog have a head, a nose, eyes, ears, a body, etc.) In what ways don't you and the puppy look like each other? (The puppy is smaller than the children, has four legs instead of two, has hair all over its body, has a tail, etc.)
Can you think of things that a puppy might learn from its mother and father?
Pretend that the puppy is yours. Can you think of things that it might learn from you as it grows up into a dog?
Can you think of things you might learn from a dog? (Responses could be amusing here, including turning around several times before lying down and chasing cats. And answers could be serious, such as learning to develop and use the sense of smell to a greater degree.)
Might a dog learn things by living with one person or family that it might not learn by living with another person or family? Why, or why not? Could a dog raised in the city learn some things that it might not learn if it were raised in the country? Why, or why not? Could a dog raised in the country learn some things that it might not learn if it were raised in the city? Why, or why not? Could a dog living with the people of one society learn some things that it might not learn by living with the people of another society? Why, or why not? If a dog were to be moved from one society to another, might it have to unlearn some things and learn other things? Why, or why not?
All right. So far, we have just shared our feelings without really checking any of our facts. But, right now, do you believe that dogs could have a "culture" of their own? Why, or why not? Do you believe that a dog could learn something about the "culture" of the society in which it is raised? Why, or why not?

Would you like to try to find out now—with different animals and different peoples—whether any animals in addition to humankind have a "culture" of their own? Whether one animal might be able to learn parts of the "culture" of another? Whether humankind can learn the "culture" of other animals? Whether animals can learn something about the "culture" of human societies?

Again, the purpose of this activity is to have fun learning about the idea of culture by speculating on whether this key anthropological concept might be applied to animals in addition to humankind. Therefore, a purely fictional approach might be used to establish a relaxed, pleasant, tentative mood. From the primary grades on through the senior high school, teachers could use a variety of readily available fables, short stories, and novels which assign "human" qualities to animals and reveal something about the "cultures" of various societies through the actions and expressed beliefs of different creatures.

For example, a teacher could read aloud to a class and then invite a discussion of a passage such as the one below from *Charlotte's Web,* in which E. B. White applies human cultural values to animal characters who are members of a barnyard "society."

> ... (T)he gander opened his strong wings and beat the air with them to show his power. He was strong and brave, but the truth is, both the goose and the gander were worried about Templeton. And with good reason. The rat had no morals, no conscience, no scruples, no consideration, no decency, no milk of rodent kindness, no compunctions, no higher feeling, no friendliness, no anything. He would kill a gosling if he could get away with it—the goose knew that. Everybody knew it.[6]

In "Rikki-tikki-tavi," a story in *The Jungle Books,* written by Rudyard Kipling, the "evil" Nag threatens everyone's security and perpetuates mythology associated with the cobra. Excerpts such as this could nourish class discussion:

> "What is the matter?" asked Rikki-tikki.
> "We are very miserable," said Darzee. "One of our babies fell out of the nest yesterday and Nag ate him."
> "H'm!" said Rikki-tikki, "that is very sad—but I am a stranger here. Who is Nag?" ...
> Then inch by inch out of the grass rose up the head and spread hood of Nag, the big black cobra, and he was five feet long from tongue to tail. ...
> "Who is Nag?" said he. "I am Nag. The great God Brahm put his mark upon all our people, when the first cobra spread his hood to keep the sun off Brahm as he slept. Look, and be afraid!"[7]

A third source and an especially appropriate book from which to read aloud—with a likely appeal in grades five to eight, but with a reading level for grade seven and above—, is *Mrs. Frisby and the Rats of NIMH* by Robert C. O'Brien. In this Newbury Award-winning story, a neurologist captures a number of rats for an experiment at NIMH to see whether a program of injections might help the rodents to learn more and to learn faster. The life span of the rats is increased greatly. The rodents are taught to read, and, having mastered reading, they are able to plan their escape from NIMH. They learn more than any rats ever had previously, and they approach or exceed human intelligence. One of the rats is recalling the rodents' adventure and development in these selections:

> The reading we did! We knew very little about the world, you see, and we were curious. We learned about astronomy, about electricity, biology and mathematics, about music and art. I even read quite a few books of poetry and got to like it pretty well.
>
> Most of the books were about people; we tried to find some about rats, but there wasn't much.
>
> So we built ourselves the life you see around you. Our colony thrived and grew to one hundred fifteen. We taught our children to read and write. We had plenty to eat, running water, electricity, a fan to draw in fresh air, an elevator, a refrigerator. ...
>
> And yet here we were, rats getting caught up in something a lot like the People Race, and for no good reason. ... [8]

The fourth and last book in this short series could be read by highly motivated senior high school students. However, by carefully selecting certain passages to read aloud in class, teachers in the intermediate grades and above might use *Watership Down* by Richard Adams. In this touching portion, the rabbit Hazel dies, survives the body, and is guided into the next world:

> ... (Hazel) raised his head and said, "Do you want to talk to me?"
> "Yes, that's what I've come for," replied the other (rabbit). "You know me, don't you?"
> "Yes, of course," said Hazel, hoping he would be able to remember his name in a moment. Then he saw that in the darkness of the burrow the stranger's ears were shining with a faint silver light. "Yes, my lord," he said. "Yes, I know you."
> "You've been feeling tired," said the stranger, "but I can do something about that. I've come to ask whether you'd care to join my Owsla (the strongest rabbits in a warren). We shall be glad to have you and you'll enjoy it. If you're ready, we might go along now."
> ... It seemed to Hazel that he would not be needing his body any more, so he left it lying on the edge of the ditch, but stopped for a moment to watch his rabbits and to try to get used to the extraordinary feeling that strength and speed were flowing inexhaustibly out of him into their sleek young bodies and healthy senses.
> "You needn't worry about them," said his companion. "They'll be all right—and thousands like them. If you'll come along, I'll show you what I mean." [9]

The second set of reading materials also consists of four books, *Julie of the Wolves, Gentle Ben, Incident at Hawk's Hill,* and *White Fang.* These novels are concerned with people *and* animals, as animals, in fictional, but natural, true-to-life settings. At this point, the teacher would guide a class toward more serious, substantial questions concerning whether some animals might have a "culture" of their own, whether—if certain animals *do* have a "culture"—humankind can learn portions of animal "culture," and whether other animals can learn aspects of the cultures of various peoples.

Winner of the 1973 Newbery Medal, *Julie of the Wolves* is likely to be enjoyed immediately, appreciated readily, and discussed easily and meaningfully by learners in grades four through eight. The book's author, Jean Craighead George, is a naturalist who has made first-hand observations of wolves. She also demonstrates a feeling for Eskimo culture. The central character in the story is a thirteen-year-old girl whose name is Julie in English and Miyax in Eskimo. During the time Julie lives with the wolves, she learns behavior they expect of her and sees the young being taught. In this instance, the teacher might read the entire story aloud to the class and then pause for interaction on passages such as these:

> ... Miyax was lost. She had been lost without food for many sleeps on the North Slope of Alaska.... (T)he very life in her body, its spark and warmth, depended upon these wolves for survival. ...
>
> Miyax stared hard at the regal black wolf, hoping to catch his eye. She must somehow tell him that she was starving and ask him for food. This could be done she knew, for her father, an Eskimo hunter, had done so. ...
>
> ... Rehearsing whimpers and groveling positions as she climbed to her lookout, she got ready to tell Amaroq how helpless she was in his own language.
>
> "Ayi!" she gasped. On the side of a ground swell lay Jello, his body torn in bloody shreds, his face contorted. Beside him lay her backpack!
>
> Instantly she knew what had happened. Amaroq had turned on him. Once Kapugen had told her that some wolves had tolerated a lone wolf until the day he stole meat from the pups. With that, the leader gave a signal and his pack turned, struck, and tore the lone wolf to pieces. "There is no room in the wolf society for an animal who cannot contribute," he had said.
>
> ... Miyax rocked back on her heels. Could it be that the leader of the pack was teaching the leader of the pups? She nodded slowly as she comprehended. Of course. To be a leader required not only fearlessness and intelligence, but experience and schooling. The head of a wolf pack needed to be trained, and who better to do this than Amaroq?[10]

At the intermediate, middle school, and junior high school levels, Walt Morey's well-known *Gentle Ben* is useful, for the bear is raised in captivity, turned loose to make it in the wild, and then brought into contact with humankind again, as the following selections reveal:

> Ben had much to learn. The years he had spent chained in a shed had made him a complete stranger to the wild. Now, with his first taste of freedom, he set out to explore this new and wonderful land. ...
>
> "... He's spent a winter alone in the wild. He hasn't seen a human being in months. And this spring you can bet your life he's fought other brownies for fishing rights on that stream. If I'm any judge, Ben now has the finest fishing spot on the creek. Ben has forgotten his tame-bear days. You can bet on that. He's now a wild brownie in every sense of the word."[11]

The third book in this set, *Incident at Hawk's Hill* by Allan W. Eckert, can be read aloud to and discussed by learners in grades five through twelve. The story takes place in 1870 near Winnipeg, and an author's note states that it is "a slightly fictionalized version of an incident which actually occurred at the time and place noted." In the book, six-year-old Ben MacDonald strays from his home, gets lost, encounters a storm, finds refuge in a badger's tunnel, is mothered by the female badger over a period of time, and takes the badger with him when he is finally found and returned to the family farm. *Incident at Hawk's Hill* is perfect for the purpose here, as excerpts such as those below almost compel pupils to talk about whether the boy may have learned the badger's "culture" and whether the badger may have learned facets of the boy's culture.

Though the relationship between boy and badger had begun simply as one of food and shelter, it did not remain that way. A deep affection was developing between them and a spirit of play as well....

Frequently they played a sort of tag. She would run from him and he would scramble after her through the tall grasses, panting and giggling at one point, wheezing and chattering at another. And when at last he would catch her—or she would *let* him catch her—he would tackle her around the middle and they would roll over and over together, their snarlings and growlings of mock battle intermingling. Suddenly it would be his turn and he would dash away with her closing in behind him and she would pounce upon him in much the same manner and once again they would wrestle amidst giggles and chatterings.

By the beginning of his third week with her, Ben was astonishingly badger-like in all he did. He could keep up with her reasonably well and he grunted and wheezed as he waddled along, just as she did. He was no longer so particular about what he would eat and devoured with equal alacrity any prey she brought to him, including frogs and lemmings and once even a small red-bellied snake. ... His night vision was becoming extremely good and he almost seemed to prefer it to daylight. His mental clock became turned around and, like the female badger, he slept most of the day and was alert most of the night.

There was no doubt that the big female badger had adopted him in place of her pups which had died while she was trapped. It was evident that she was bringng food to him and attempting to train him in hunting just as she would have done her own young. It was considerably more difficult, however, to understand the change in the boy. Except in his habits of defecation and urination, Ben MacDonald had virtually ceased being a human being and was adapting incredibly well to this life of a badger.

Now it was Ben—cleaned and doctored and recuperating well under Esther's care—who cared for the badger, feeding her and protecting her as she had done for him at the den. She adapted remarkably well to his way of life. ...

For a week Ben alternated between two lives, sometimes running around on all fours, growling, hissing, chattering and tussling with the badger as they played a sort of King-of-the-Hill game on the the earth pile near the house where the well was being dug, and at other times talking with his family and acting like any other little boy his age....[12]

Jack London's *White Fang* fits beautifully into this group, too. Children and young adults should enjoy discussing London's vivid description of the process by which a wolf is tamed into the likeness of a dog and instructed in elements of human culture. Here are some of the lines that students might contemplate from an anthropological point of view:

...The master's voice was sufficient. By it White Fang knew whether he did right or not. By it he trimmed his conduct and adjusted his actions. It was the compass by which he steered and learned to chart the manners of a new land and life.

But it was the multiplicity of laws that befuddled White Fang and often brought him into disgrace. He had to learn that he must not touch the chickens that belonged to other gods. Then there were cats, and rabbits, and turkeys; all these he must let alone. In fact, when he had but partly learned the law, his impression was that he must leave all live things alone. . . .

. . . In the end, the master laughed him out of his dignity. His jaws slightly parted, his lips lifted a little, a quizzical expression that was more love than humor came into his eyes. He had learned to laugh.

Likewise he learned to romp with the master, to be tumbled down and rolled over, and be the victim of innumerable rough tricks. . . . This would always culminate with the master's arms going around White Fang's neck and shoulders while the latter crooned and growled his love-song.[13]

A third and final set of sources could include nonfiction works by wildlife photographers, animal trainers, veterinarians, naturalists, biologists, psychologists, and others. Following the format already established here, the teacher could read aloud to the entire class from and invite a discussion of books such as *Gifts of an Eagle, Never Cry Wolf, In the Shadow of Man,* and *Lucy: Growing Up Human: A Chimpanzee Daughter in a Psychotherapist's Family.*

Or, the teacher could encourage students to form five to eight committees around given animals that they have selected. The committee investigating dogs and the idea of culture, for instance, could consult books including *Why Does Your Dog Do That?*[14] Each of the committees might be responsible for planning and executing a report, a panel, a symposium, a forum, and the like.

Or, with all of the relevant sources that are available in many places, each learner could do independent study on an animal, topic, or problem of interest to him or her, such as "Do Bottle-Nosed Dolphins Have—and/or Can They Learn—a 'Language?' " Highly motivated and gifted high school students might examine more scholarly sources[15] to see where their reading leads them.

The first of the of the four books that the teacher could use for oral reading followed by the interaction of class members is *Gifts of an Eagle,* written by Kent Durden. Durden has a bachelor's degree in biology and has become a wildlife photographer and a lecturer for the National Audubon Society. Motion picture film footage of Lady, the golden eagle described by Durden, appeared on the Walt Disney and the "Lassie" television shows. Lady was captured as a nestling and brought up by Kent Durden and his father. Her attempt to raise a gosling as an eagle is one of the most amusing, intriguing, and anthropologically germane parts of the book:

. . . An idea began to germinate in Dad's mind. When he first saw her eggs, he was struck with their resemblance in size to the domestic goose egg. Would she accept a replacement of a fertile goose egg for her own? It was worth a try.

. . . The gosling had adapted to this foreign way of feeding and was now eating like an eagle. This was just the first of many adaptations both eagle and gosling were to undergo as this unique youngster grew.

By midsummer the goose was full grown. Lady still provided his food, but now he would tear into meat as ferociously as an eagle, and he could do remarkably well with the tools he was equipped with. Though he was fed primarily on vegetation, he never turned down the chance for flesh food. A visitor who might happen to see the goose tearing into a jackrabbit, or as on one occasion, trying to swallow a snake, might be hard to convince that we weren't experimenting with a secret drug that would change all mice into lions.[16]

Never Cry Wolf, the second nonfiction work recommended for this set, is informative, insightful, and *funny!* The author, Farley Mowat, is a naturalist, biologist, ethnologist, and novelist. Learners in grades six through twelve should enjoy listening to material such as the following and then talking about its relevance to the idea of culture:

> One factor concerning the organization of the family mystified me very much at first. During my early visit to the den I had seen *three* adult wolves...
> Whoever the third wolf was, he was definitely a character. ... He became "Uncle Albert" to me after the first time I saw him with the pups.
> The sixth morning of my vigil had dawned bright and sunny, and Angeline and the pups took advantage of the good weather. Hardly was the sun risen (at three A.M.) when they all left the den and adjourned to a nearby sandy knoll. Here the pups worked over their mother with an enthusiasm which would certainly have driven any human female into hysterics. They were hungry; but they were also full to the ears with hellery. Two of them did their best to chew off Angeline's tail, worrying it and fighting over it until I thought I could actually see her fur flying like spindrift; while the other two did what they could to remove her ears.
>
> Eventually she gave it up. Harrassed beyond endurance she leaped away from her brood and raced to the top of a high sand ridge behind the den. The four pups rolled cheerfully off in pursuit, but before they could reach her she gave vent to a most peculiar cry.
> The whole question of wolf communications was to intrigue me more and more as time went on, but on this occasion I was still laboring under the delusion that complex communications among animals other than man did not exist. I could make nothing definite of Angeline's high-pitched and yearning whine-cum howl. I did, however, detect a plaintive quality in it which made my sympathies go out to her.
> I was not alone. Within seconds of her *cri-de-coeur,* and before the mob of pups could reach her, a savior appeared.
> It was the third wolf.... He... trotted straight toward the den—intercepting the pups as they prepared to scale the last slope to reach their mother.
> I watched, fascinated, as he used his shoulder to bowl the leading pup over on its back and send it skidding down the lower slope toward the den. Having broken the charge, he then nipped another pup lightly on its fat behind; then he shepherded the lot of them back to what I later came to recognize as the playground area.
> I hesitate to put human words into a wolf's mouth, but the effect of what followed was crystal clear. "If it's a workout you kids want," he might have said, "then I'm your wolf!"
> And so he was. For the next hour he played with the pups with as much energy as if he were still one himself. The games were varied, but many of them were quite recognizable. Tag was the standby, and Albert was always "it." Leaping, rolling and weaving amongst the pups, he never left the area of the nursery knoll, while at the same time leading the youngsters such a chase that they eventually gave up.[17]

In the Shadow of Man is Jane van Lawick-Goodall's story of her ten years among the wild chimpanzees of Tanzania. The teacher might use these excerpts to stimulate an exchange of ideas:

> At the Gombe Stream alone we have seen chimpanzees use objects for many different purposes. They use stems and sticks to capture and eat insects and, if the material picked is not suitable, then it is modified. They use leaves to sop up water they cannot reach with

their lips, and first they chew on the leaves and thus increase their absorbency. . . . They sometimes use sticks as levers to enlarge underground bees' nests.

. . . (I)t seems almost certain that, although the ability to manipulate objects is innate in a chimpanzee, the actual tool-using patterns practiced by the Gombe Stream chimpanzees are learned by infants from their elders. We saw one very good example of this. It happened when a female had diarrhea: she picked a large handful of leaves and wiped her messy bottom. Her two-year-old infant watched her closely and then twice picked leaves and wiped his own clean bottom.[18]

Finally, a virtually irresible book for the purpose here is *Lucy: Growing Up Human: A Chimpanzee Daughter in a Psychotherapist's Family* by Maurice K. Temerlin. Below are representative selections that could be discussed:

Removed from her mother shortly after birth, Lucy was taken into our home and raised as much as possible as though she were a human being. From birth to maturity she never saw another chimpanzee, so that she could learn whatever she learned only from human beings. . . .

. . . We did not have to teach her to use spoons or forks. She would see us using silverware and immediately do so herself. . . . By the time she was 15 months old she seemed quite comfortable with all the paraphernalia with which humans consume their food. . . .

The signs Lucy learned (According to Dr. Roger Fouts, who taught Lucy the American Sign Language for the Deaf (ASL), after 4½ years of training and at the age of 9½ years, Lucy had a vocabulary of around 100 words.) gave her a conceptual and communicative tool. She now asks questions about her environment. As she sees something new she often asks "What's that?" by moving a forefinger rapidly left and right *(what)* and then pointing the same forefinger at the object to be identified *(that)*. She asks this question of us, and at times of herself, as she leafs through a magazine and sees something she has not seen before. . . .

. . . This conversation ensued, Lucy speaking ASL while I replied in English.
Lucy: "Tickle Lucy."
Maury: "No! I'm busy."
Lucy: "Chase Lucy."
Maury: "Not now."
Lucy: "Hug Lucy, hurry, hurry."
Maury: "In just a minute."
Lucy: (Laughing): "Hurry, hurry, hug Lucy, tickle, chase Lucy."
How could I resist?[19]

Using Words to Learn More about Culture

Through a variety of social studies learning activities related to anthropology, many learners in elementary and secondary schools are likely to gain some feeling for the importance of language as an ingredient in culture. This portion of the chapter has been developed to give learners more direct experiences with words and cultural meanings they connote.

In chapter 5, Pelto says that because the Inuit's lives are greatly influenced by different kinds of snow, these important variations must be characterized by separate words. Might this phenomenon be found in other cultures and subcultures? The teacher could introduce the significance of word shadings by giving a "test" to learners in grades four through twelve. On a sheet of lined paper, each class member might be asked to write all the following items and then to identify them briefly.

AIR BEAR	GRASSHOPPER
BIG HAT	KODIAK WITH A KODAK
CITY KITTY	LOCAL YOKEL
COUNTRY JOE	MAMMA SMOKEY
COUNTY MOUNTY	NIGHT CRAWLERS
EVEL KNIEVEL SMOKEY	WHITE RABBIT WITH EARS

After everyone has had adequate time to take the "ID test," the teacher could invite a class discussion on the students' efforts to define the words. Then, the teacher could explain that the words appear in *The Official CB Slanguage Language Dictionary* by Lanie Dills[20] in which they are defined in alphabetical order as "police in helicopter," "state trooper," "local police," "rural police," "Sheriff's Department," "motorcycle police," "park policeman," "police with radar," "local police," "female state trooper," "police everywhere," and "police with CB." Next, the teacher might ask students to respond to questions such as these:

Why do you think that truckers and drivers of automobiles with CB radios use so many different words for officers of the law?
Can you suggest your own examples of other things in the United States for which we have a number of words with special meanings?
In our state or other states?
In our city or other cities?
In our community or other communities?
In this neighborhood or other neighborhoods?
In this school or other schools?
In your home or other homes?
Now, what about cultures and subcultures in other countries? Might there be some things with important differences that require more than one name? If you cannot think of possibilities now, would you like to have some independent study time to work on such an activity in our classroom, in the school library, or in the media center?

Assuming that learners respond to the independent study opportunity just offered, the teacher might help individual pupils with ideas and materials, encourage students to assist each other, and suggest that class members consult with their parents, friends, neighbors, and other teachers. After every learner has identified and investigated an idea, the teacher could let each person decide how she or he would like to report her or his findings. Some individuals might prefer to confer with the teacher and just tell what they learned. Others might write reports solely for the teacher. Still others might be willing to share their discoveries with the entire class, through oral reports, articles for a class magazine, bulletin board displays, slide presentations, exhibits of realia, and other means.

Below are examples of imaginary oral reports that reveal what two motivated senior high school students might uncover and contribute.

I'm taking French II with "Mademoiselle" Francophile this year. I asked her if she could help me come up with a thing that the French people have different words for. She said she'd have to think about it a day or two. She's been to France twice in the summer, you know. Anyway, later she said maybe I could do something with French cooking. She said that the French people really have a thing, for instance, about sauces. They say, "La sauce c'est tout." That means that the sauce is everything. So, Ms. Francophile loaned me *Mastering the Art of French Cooking*[21] by Julia Child, and she told me to see what I could find out.

It looks to me like the French have *groups* of sauces, like white sauces— called *sauces blanches*—, brown sauces—*sauces brunes*—, tomato sauces—*sauces tomate*—, then *hollandaise* sauces, and kinds of *mayonnaise*, and oil and vinegar sauces—or *vinaigrettes*—, and hot butter sauces—*sauces au beurre*—, and stuff like that. Sauces in some of the groups have names like *béarnaise, béchamel, bordelaise, madère, mornay, remoulade,* and *tartare.* Béarnaise sauce got its name from "Béarn," a district in the southwest of France. Béarnaise is a sauce with egg yolks, shallots—kinda like small onions—, butter, vinegar, and other things. There are even different kinds of béarnaise sauce, would you believe? One, called *colbert,* is béarnaise sauce with a meat glaze flavoring. Another, *choron,* has a tomato flavoring.

"Mademoiselle" Franchophile says that a French cook can spend most of a day getting a nice sauce ready. Many French people, taxi drivers and all, know the names of a lot of sauces. People often take their time eating an evening meal in France. A lot of times, only one course is served at a time with its own special sauce.

My French teacher says a lot of Americans don't know or care about cooking and don't appreciate dishes that have been prepared slowly and carefully. We want a lot of food, served and eaten in a hurry. We dump catsup on all sorts of things, and it covers up the real flavor of the food. We make only a few kinds of gravy—usually in a hurry too—, and our gravy is often heavy and greasy and lumpy. We just say, "Please pass the gravy" instead of, "May I please have the 'sauce ragoût?' "

*   *   *   *   *

You're not going to believe this! I went to Miss Francophile too! I couldn't get started! She said she could work with me if I could find a way to see her during her only period for planning and for conferences. It turns out that I have study hall then, so I spent most of one period talking with her.

"Mademoiselle" Francophile suggested that I check into French bread— *pain français.* She said that she'd spent more time in neighborhood bakeries in Lyons than in other cities in France. She isn't sure that everything she told me is true all over the country.

Well, Ms. Francophile says the people in Lyons care so much about their freshly baked bread that they buy it daily, even two or three times! Like Americans say, "Good as gold," the French say, "Bon comme le bon pain," or

"Good like good bread." They also say, "Un repas sans pain est comme un jour sans soleil." That means, "A meal without bread is like a day without sunshine." See how important bread is to them?

Oh, I should slip something in here before I forget it. Miss Francophile says that the French bread I'm going to talk about doesn't have any preservatives in it to keep it from spoiling, like a bunch of American bread does. So, the French bread doesn't stay fresh long or keep well; it just tastes great!

But the thing I found out that relates to what we're studying in this class is that the French have a lot of names for the *shape* of French bread. I mean, you wouldn't bounce into a French bakery and say, "Hey, I'd like a loaf of bread." You would ask for *une ficelle, baguette, flute, miche, couronne,* and like that, according to Miss Francophile. The *Ficelle* is long and thin like a piece of rope or string. The *baguette* is the same length as the *ficelle,* but the *baguette* is thicker. The *flute* is thicker and shorter than the *baguette.* The *miche* is round. The *couronne* is shaped like a crown. "Mademoiselle" Francophile let me borrow a book[22] that shows pictures of some of the shapes of French bread and has even more names, like *joko, boulot,* and *pain de campagne.* It also gives examples of three shapes of rolls. But the French don't call them "rolls." They say, *"petits pains,"* or "little breads." One of the *petits pains* is called *champignon* and looks like a mushroom. Another, *pistolet,* means pistol. A third, which looks like a corkscrew, is ordered in French as *tire-bouchon.*

It would be hard to find out in countries all over the world, but I wonder if the number of words people have for something might give you a clue on how important it is for them. But, I suppose it's not that simple. Anyway, the French sure have a bunch of names for the shape of their bread.

Obviously, the faculty members in any elementary or secondary school can greatly enrich each other's teaching by continually sharing ideas with respect to sound objectives, meaningful content, effective methods, appropriate instructional materials, and facilitative evaluation procedures. Social studies teachers who are not as well rounded in English and foreign language as certain of their colleagues should request assistance. The basic idea here is to encourage elementary and secondary learners to examine words that Americans have adopted and adapted from other cultures and words that have been created in the United States and added to the vocabularies of various peoples. This would be an especially good place, of course, to introduce or reinforce an understanding of cultural diffusion, for langauge is a cultural element which has been transmitted back and forth in many parts of the world.

Using a dictionary that includes the derivations of words, the teacher could select common and uncommon words with interesting and varied sources and stories. Each word would be lettered on a separate 3"x 5" card. The teacher might place 30-40 cards in a small recipe box to begin this activity. Words such as those below could be used initially. (Only the words themselves would appear on the cards, of course, but in brackets I have indicated one source for each word to emphasize the heterogeneity of our American vocabulary and to indicate what learners might discover.)

apple [Old English]	house [German]
bagel [Yiddish]	karate [Japanese]
beaver [Lithuanian]	kowtow [Chinese]
boy [Old High German]	marimba [West African]
bridge [Icelandic]	opossum [Algonquin]
calendar [Anglo-French]	orange [Sanskrit]
candy [Persian]	paprika [Hungarian]
cat [Celtic]	parka [Russian]
chocolate [Nahautl]	piano [Italian]
clown [Danish]	picnic [French]
compass [Vulgar Latin]	plaza [Spanish]
cookie [Dutch]	rabbit [Flemish]
coyote [Mexican Spanish]	ring [Old Icelandic]
democracy [Greek]	table [Latin]
dog [Middle English]	taboo [Polynesian]
dolphin [Old Provençal]	tam [Scottish]
fish [Gothic]	ugly [Old Norse]
flat [Swedish]	whiskey [Gaelic]
flower [Old French]	yogurt [Turkish]
guru [Hindi]	yoke [Hittite]

Pupils who "get done early" with other class activities, who want to earn extra credit, who are fascinated by words, and/or who need frequent and varied challenges, can select cards from the teacher's recipe box and can enter their findings on the cards so they can be read and enjoyed by classmates. Students can also letter intriguing and humorous words on cards to spur their peers. And learners can identify and investigate their own words. Here, for example, is what a class member might write on his or her card, which would then go into the recipe box for others to read:

ARCTIC

"Arctic" comes from the Greek word *arktos*. It means "bear." *Arktikos* is the name of the Great Bear constellation in the northern part of the world.
So, when you think of the arctic, you can think of a big white bear.[23]

As soon as learners have some awarness of the number and variety of words Americans have borrowed from other cultures, the teacher might help pupils to see that certain words we use frequently have been absorbed elsewhere. For instance, below are some Hispanicized English words[24] with which learners in the intermediate grades and above could have fun. Using the chalkboard or flash cards, the teacher could display one word at a time in New Mexican Spanish and give each student an opportunity to try to come up with the English word from which it has been derived. (Again, just the words would be displayed, but I have indicated in brackets what participants might discover.)

airopuerto [airport]
baicico [bicycle]
balun [balloon]
bebe [baby]
caite [kite]
claun [clown]
dipo [depot]
dres [dress]
drinque [drink]
fayaman [fireman]
fone [funny]
fútbol [football]
garache [garage]
grocerías [groceries]
jaihue [highway]

lonche [lunch]
overajoles [overalls]
panqueque [pancake]
pare [party]
payamas [pajamas]
piquinique [picnic]
plis [please]
queque [cake]
rede [ready]
saihuaque [sidewalk]
sanhuichi [sandwich]
suera [sweater]
torque [turkey]
troca [truck]
yele [jelly]

After a senior high school social studies teacher has displayed one Hispanicized English word at a time, she or he might like to provide students with an entire paragraph for a context in which American-English words have been adopted, as is, for use in another culture. Having secured the publisher's permission, the teacher might reproduce the delightful example below, give each class member a copy, and ask everyone to underline those words that the French have borrowed from our everyday vocabulary.

Comment trouver un parking pendant le week-end? Ce n'est pas facile et Michelle commencait `s'impatienter. Elle avait rendezvous avec son boy-friend, Alain, au club de ping-pong, et elle était déjà en retard parce qu'elle avait faite du baby-sitting pour sa soeur. Le club se trouvait dans un building de grand standing. Elle avait juste le temps de faire un peu de shopping avant de retrouver Alain. Elle avait envie de s'acheter un blue-jeans et un sweater. Alain trouvait cela sexy...Ensuite Alain lui offrirait un cocktail au club et ils iraient au dancing. Elle était impatiente de savoir le résultat de l'interview d'Alain avec le patron d'une agence de voyages. Il avait tant envie de ce job de guide! Et avec l'argent qu'il gagnerait, ils pourraient aller manger au snack-bar toutes les fois qu'il le voudraient. Lui predrait sans doute un hamburger avec beaucoup de ketchup et un hot-dog; elle du caté et une apple pie. Ce serait la belle vie![25]

Still another way that an enterprising, creative elementary or secondary social studies teacher can use words to help children or youth learn more about culture is to employ interesting, entertaining, amusing, informative, sensitive, and inspirational riddles, proverbs, poems, song lyrics, folktales, myths, legends, ritual orations, and prayers. There are numerous, varied, and readily available sources, which could be tapped here. The teacher could read aloud to the class, encourage learners to read privately and aloud to each other and to the class, ask for volunteers to print and illustrate favorite selections for bulletin board displays, assist small groups in preparing and performing musical numbers, dances, skits, and plays, and so on. The possibilities here are almost endless on a K-12 basis, and only a *few* examples of specific sources are provided here.

Riddles can intrigue and amuse learners, and those assembled in *Ji-Nongo-Nongo Means Riddles* by Verna Aardema are ideal for the anthropological perspective envisioned here. Incidentally, Aardema's books based on African folklore, including *Tales from the Story Hat, Why Mosquitoes Buzz in People's Ears,* and *Who's in Rabbit's House,* would work beautifully in the folklore area. The following are riddles from the Yoruba, Ga, Kanuri, and Hausa cultures, which learners may find especially appealing:

Yoruba
Who has a house too small for guests?
Answer: The tortoise
Ga
What leaps down the mountain, but cannot climb back up?
Answer: The mountain stream.
Kanuri
What is it that even the ostrich with its long neck and sharp eyes cannot see?
Answer: What will happen tomorrow.
Hausa
What lies down when it's hungry and stands up when it's full?
Answer: A rice sack.[26]

Another view of cultures and the words they use could be gained by an examination of proverbs, to see what popular sayings might reveal about needs, interests, problems, beliefs, and aspirations of humankind in general and cultures and individuals in those cultures in particular. To introduce a class to activities involving aphorisms, the teacher could start with examples selected from "Proverbs," Chapter 15 in *The Maasai* by S. S. Sankan. Sankan presents a numbered list of Maasai statements of truths in the form of a literal translation and then in an interpreted version.

1	One finger does not kill a flea.	1	A man is helpless while alone; unity is strength.
29	A dog cannot keep watch on two homes.	29	You should not attempt to do two things simultaneously.
94	An earthquake does not cease until it has seen another one.	94	A strong thing can only be countermanded by a strong one.
145	You cannot force water up a hill.	145	Certain things are impossible to achieve.
166	Do not sweep someone else's house while yours is dirty.	166	Correct yourself before you correct others.

Next, the teacher might select one of Sankan's simplified proverbs for each class member and invite every learner to see if he or she can match the Maasai aphorism with a quotable quotation used by Americans. The following illustrations suggest possibilities:

Maasai Proverbs
13 A man never forgets his original home.

American Proverbs
You can take the boy out of Oregon (away from the farm, etc.), but you can never take Oregon out of the boy (man).

18	You do not miss that which you have, but as soon as it is taken away from you, then you begin seeing its value.	You never miss the water till the well runs dry.
23	One cannot give up one's habits that were developed in childhood.	As the twig is bent, the tree's inclined.
79	Take one step at a time.	Take one step at a time.
97	You cannot get anything for nothing.	You don't get something for nothing.
105	Do not bet on a thing before you know its nature.	Don't count your chickens before they hatch.
112	A small thing can develop.	Big oaks from little acorns grow.
117	Small drops fill an ocean.	Every little bit helps.
135	To be slow and sure is preferable to being fast and unsure.	Plodding wins the race.
156	Actions speak louder than words.	Actions speak louder than words.
191	One good deed deserves another.	One good deed deserves another.
194	Do not throw the baby out with the dirty bathwater.[27]	Don't throw the baby out with the bath water.

Teachers from the primary grades on through senior high school can easily locate many poems—written in English and available in translation—from numerous cultures. For instance, *Miracles: Poems by Children of the English-Speaking World* is an excellent collection of almost 200 poems, written by authors between the ages of five and fourteen from Australia, Canada, England, India, Ireland, Kenya, New Zealand, the Philippines, Uganda, and the United States. Using sources similar to *Miracles,* each learner could be encouraged to read a variety of poems and then to select one poem about which he or she might write or draw his or her feelings. Or, the entire class might discuss portions or entire poems such as these:

I walk to school
beside my friend.
Our gray-blue uniforms
as neat as the petals of a flower.
But all I see in difference is
that my girlfriend has another name.
Noelene Qualthrough
Age 11
Australia

My Old Grandfather
My old grandfather is dead and buried.
An orange tree was planted over his grave.
The tree fed on him and grew taller.
The oranges grew ripe and ready to drop.
The wind came and blew them off.
I came, picked them up and ate.
O what a dreadful thing!
I ate my poor grandfather's body.
Joseph Alumasa
Age 14
Kenya[28]

The lyrics of folksongs, ballads, marches, hymns, and anthems can be tremen-
dously moving and enlightening and can give learners a real feeling for both the
diversity and the unity of humankind. Here, for example, are the lyrics of a Tupi love
song, found in *In the Trail of the Wind: American Indian Poems and Ritual Orations*,
edited by John Bierhorst, which might be appropriate in innumerable cultures:

> New Moon, O New Moon,
> Remind that man of me!
> Here am I in your presence;
> Cause it to be that only I
> Shall occupy his heart.[29]

Two folktales have been included here for illustrative purposes. The story of
Akomunyana, which follows, is from the Bunyoro culture of Uganda. Class members
might compare it with the Wolf Man tales and films with which they are familiar.

> Once upon a time there was a herdsman who became prosperous and accumulated a
> large herd of cattle. He also had a large family with a fairly large number of children.
> Among his children there was a very beautiful daughter who besides being beautiful was
> rather mischievous and kept getting herself into trouble. One day when her turn came to
> take the calves out to feed, (she) took them to pasture and as she passed a rocky stretch of
> ground she saw a pool of beautiful clear water. Suddenly she had an urge to drink some of
> it which she proceeded to do. She did not know that a lion had urinated there. As soon as
> she finished drinking, the girl felt her whole body heave and change. Then she realized
> she had turned into a lion. She rushed at the calves caught and killed one of them and ate
> it....From then on this practice of turning into a lion became frequent especially at the
> time of the new moon!...[30]

In *Never Cry Wolf,* mentioned earlier in this chapter, Faley Mowat recalls the story
of Ootek, an inland Eskimo:

> The wolf and the caribou were so closely linked, (Ootek) told me, that they were almost
> a single entity. He explained what he meant by telling me a story which sounded a little
> like something out of the Old Testament; but which, so Mike assured me, was a part of the
> semi-religious folklore of the inland Eskimos ...
> Here, paraphrased, is Ootek's tale.
> "In the beginning there was a Woman and a Man, and nothing else walked or swam or
> flew in the world until one day the Woman dug a great hole in the ground and began
> fishing in it. One by one she pulled out all the animals, and the last one she pulled out of
> the hole was the caribou. Then Kaila, who is the God of the Sky, told the woman the
> caribou was the greatest gift of all, for the caribou would be the sustenance of man.
> "The Woman set the caribou free and ordered it to go out over the land and multiply,
> and the caribou did as the Woman said; and in time the land was filled with caribou, so the
> sons of the Woman hunted well, and they were fed and clothed and had good skin tents to
> live in, all from the caribou.
> "The sons of the Woman hunted only the big, fat caribou, for they had no wish to kill
> the weak and the small and the sick, since these were no good to eat, nor were their skins
> much good. And, after a time, it happened that the sick and the weak came to outnumber
> the fat and the strong, and when the sons saw this they were dismayed and they
> complained to the Woman.

"Then the Woman made magic and spoke to Kaila and said: 'Your work is no good, for the caribou grow weak and sick, and if we eat them we must grow weak and sick also.'

"Kaila heard, and he said 'My work is good. I shall tell Amorak (the spirit of the Wolf), and he shall tell his children, and they will eat the sick and the weak and the small caribou, so that the land will be left for the fat and the good ones.'

"And this is what happened, and this why the caribou and the wolf are one; for the caribou feeds the wolf, but it is the wolf who keeps the caribou strong." [31]

The words in prayers, too, can provide learners with valuable anthropological insights, and a Bantu, a Tungus, and a Sioux prayer, follow, respectively, as examples.

Offering
Mulungu, here is your food.
We wish for rain, for wives, for cattle and
for goats to raise;
And we pray God that our people do not die
from sickness.

To the Polar Sun
O sun!
Permit us to pass our days prosperously;
Do not abandon us in the future,
Until the warm spring breezes come!

Warrior's Vow
I promise thee a calico shirt and a dress, O
Wakanda. I will also give you a blanket if you
grant that I return whole and well to my fireside
after having killed a Pawnee. [32]

Inviting Learners to Become Amateur Anthropologists

Perhaps there is a potential "anthropologist" in almost every person, ready to be discovered, encouraged, and developed. Surely many children, youth, and adults have felt something of a "sociocultural anthropological tug" while seeing a next-door neighbor respond to the actions of a toddler or a teenager, while sitting and watching the behavior (including the gestures and facial expressions) of strangers passing on the mall of a large shopping center, while listening to the speech (including a dialect or an "accent") of those in an adjacent booth in a restaurant during a vacation trip, while attending the wedding of a friend whose religious beliefs and practices are unfamiliar, and the like. Certainly individuals of various ages have experienced an "archaeological stirring" when emptying the contents of a box in the attic or a barrel in the garage at the home of grandparents, when touching a dust-covered horse collar in an old barn used only for storage a decade or more, when walking through a junkyard cluttered with parts of makes of automobiles no longer manufactured, when browsing in an antique shop, and so on.

The elementary or secondary teacher who would like to give learners a feeling for and to stimulate an interest in amateur anthropology might begin by using the letters, diaries, reports, memoirs, and autobiographies of explorers, travelers, cartographers, emissaries, pioneers, early nonprofessional ethnographers, diplomats, engineers, teachers, nurses, doctors, Peace Corps workers, and others. The teacher could read excerpts aloud to a class and/or help each student to select something compelling to study independently.

The personal accounts of Indian captives are unusually fascinating and fit in especially well with American history, often offered in grades five, eight, and eleven. One such description has been published in an attractive edition by the Ohio Historical Society as SCOOUWA: *James Smith's Indian Captivity Narrative*. Before reading Smith's words, the teacher could share with pupils portions of the introductory matter, such as these:

> James Smith was born in 1737...At the age of eighteen, in 1755, he was taken captive by the Indians, was adopted into one of their families, and accompanied them in all their wanderings, till his escape in 1759. ...
>
> ... Smith's sensitive yet unemotional captivity journal illustrates man's basic struggle for survival in an unbroken wilderness: the precarious lives of the Indians, the European influences on their customs and dress... As Smith's journal evolves, his captors become more than brutal tomahawk-swinging scalp collectors for he reveals the varied dimensions of Indian customs and culture....[33]

Then, the teacher might read aloud to a class excerpts such as the following:

> ... (The Indians) took me prisoner. The one that laid hold on me was a Canasatauga, the other two were Delawares. One of them could speak English...
>
> ... Though (the Delaware Indian) spoke but bad English, yet I found him to be a man of considerable understanding. ... I asked him if I should be admitted to remain with the French? He said no—and told me that as soon as I recovered (from a severe beating received as a result of running the gauntlet), I must not only go with the Indians, but must be made an Indian myself. ...
>
> ... (I) was then taken to an Indian town on the west branch of Muskingum, about twenty miles above the forks, which was called Tullihas, inhabited by Delawares, Caughnewagos and Mohicans. ...
>
> The day after my arrival at the aforesaid town, a number of Indians collected about me, and one of them began to pull the hair out of my head.... After this they bored my nose and ears, and fixed me off with ear rings and nose jewels, then they ordered me to strip off my clothes and put on a breech-clout, which I did; then they painted my head, face and body in various colours. ...
>
> They gave me a new ruffled shirt, which I put on, also a pair of leggins done off with ribbons and beads, likewise a pair of mockasons, and garters dressed with beads, Porcupine-quills, and redhair—also a tinsel laced cappo. They again painted my head and face with various colors, and tied a bunch of red feathers to one of these locks they had left on the crown of my head, which stood up five or six inches. They seated me on a bear skin, and gave me a pipe, tomahawk, and polecat skin pouch, which had been skinned pocket fashion, and contained tobacco, killegenico, or dry sumach leaves, which they mix with their tobacco,—also spunk, flint and steel.... —At length one of the chiefs made a speech, which was delivered to me by an interpreter,—and was as followeth:—
> "My son, you are now flesh of our flesh, and bone of our bone. By the ceremony which was performed this day, every drop of white blood was washed out of your veins; you are

taken into the Caughnewago nation, and initiated into a warlike tribe; you are adopted into a great family, and now received with great seriousness and solemnity in the room and place of a man; after what has passed this day, you are now one of us by an old strong law and custom—My son, you have now nothing to fear, we are now under the same obligations to love, support and defend you, that we are to love and to defend one another, therefore you are to consider yourself as one of your people.''...(F)rom that day I never knew them to make any distinction between me and themselves in any respect whatever until I left them—If they had plenty of clothing I had plenty, if we were scarce we all shared one fate. [34]

After the teacher has familiarized students with some lay endeavors related to sociocultural anthropology, he or she might introduce class members to the nature of professional fieldwork, provide some appropriate examples of serious studies, and then challenge learners to attempt some amateur fieldwork.

In chapter 3, Professor Pelto says that fieldwork is undoubtedly the favorite activity of anthropologists. George M. Foster and Robert V. Kemper, the editors of *Anthropologists in Cities,* support the importance of fieldwork in this statement:

> ... One principle, however, has remained constant: the anthropologist's dedication to fieldwork as his primary data-gathering strategy. Whether interested in tribal peoples, peasant villagers, or city-dwellers, anthropologists believe that the richest, most complete information on how people live comes from direct, personal participation in gathering this information. [35]

And, in *Social Anthropology in Perspective: The Relevance of Social Anthropology,* I. M. Lewis has this to say with respect to the nature of fieldwork:

> ... The modern social anthropologist relies heavily on the research procedure known as 'participant observation.' This requires him to immerse himself as thoroughly as he can in the life of the community he is trying to understand. [36]

"The center of gravity of anthropology has definitely shifted from studies outside the United States to a predominance of research closer to the home bases of anthropologists," Pelto points out in chapter 2. Foster and Kemper observe that the

> recent interest in cities is the third—and probably the final—major revolution in anthropology's definition of its subject matter. When anthropology emerged as a formal science at the end of the nineteenth century it was concerned exclusively with "primitve" (i.e., nonliterate) peoples. Then, about 1940, interest began to shift to peasant societies, the rural dimension of traditional cultures. Now, as we turn to cities, we are again on the threshold of a major change. ... [37]

Since there will be increasing anthropological research in cities, and since most students now live in urban settings, it seems appropriate that an early participant observer fieldwork experience as an amateur anthropologist could be close to home. Susan W. Byrne, did a doctoral study of an affluent retirement community in California from which the teacher might read aloud to give learners a feeling for local fieldwork possibilities. Here are just a few excerpts from "Arden (a pseudonym), an Adult Community":

... During nine months I went to meetings of thirty-two voluntary associations and interviewed leaders of fifty-seven, asking a standard set of questions concerning the origin, composition, and activities of their organizations ...

The interviews on topics other than voluntary associations were not standardized as to form or content; they were essentially one- to two-hour conversations in which I asked a great many questions. I interviewed twenty-six men and thirty-four women in this fashion, nearly always in their own apartments. In the course of each interview I requested personal information such as former occupation and place of residence, state of health, reasons for moving to Arden, features most liked and disliked about the community, relations with neighbors, ways of meeting new friends, and whereabouts of relatives. Beyond this the topics varied according to the interests and special knowledge of the informant. ...

... I attended all Arden's community events, such as arts and crafts fairs, a flea market, a Christmas party, and some of the weekly "Fun Days" — bridge party-luncheon-variety show affairs open to all residents. I gave talks about anthropology to four voluntary associations, was invited to lunch, tea, brunch, and cocktails at residents' homes, and was given recipes, plants, Christmas ornaments, articles on aging, and original poetry. ... I tried to simulate living in Arden to compensate for the shortcomings of nine-to-five ethnography. [38]

At this point, each class member could be invited to conduct his or her own brief, rather informal sociocultural anthropological "study" of a kind of "miniculture" in the community. Through the help of family and personal acquaintances, neighbors, schoolmates, friends, and relatives, the individual "researcher" could identify a group about which to learn, secure appropriate permissions, and establish a friendly, open relationship with at least one reliable, knowledgeable informant, if possible. After school and/or on weekends, the amateur field-worker could be a short-lived participant observer, gathering data and perhaps even taking photographs or slides in such a way that the dignity and privacy of individuals would not be violated. Each possible topic would be discussed in advance with the teacher to make sure that situations too sensitive for the untrained investigator could be avoided. The following are fictional titles for oral or written reports that might be suitable, interesting, and/or worthwhile:

"The Longtime Residents of the Shady Oaks Trailer Court"
"The Occupational Therapy Ward at the Valley View Memorial Hospital"
"The Communitarian Men's Civic Service Club"
"The 'Miss Zucchini' Beauty and Talent Contest"
"The Reunion of the Northside High School Class of 1960"
"The Pallino Boccie Society"
"The Workers on the Refrigerator Assembly Line at the Husky Home Appliance Company Plant #2"
"The County Fair"
"The Girls' Basketball Team at Southside High School"
"The Hyacinth Ladies' Garden Club"
"The Tranquility Nursing Home"
"The 4-Wheel Drive Volunteer Rescue Service"
"The Ruth Circle of the Central City Community Church"
"Troop 72 of the Boy Scouts of America"

A three-stage procedure similar to the one just recommended for encouraging nonprofessional sociocultural anthropologists could be employed to inspire amateur archaeologists. First, the teacher might acquaint students with the nature and importance of archaeology by reading aloud from well-written introductory books and significant, intriguing studies conducted in the past and in recent years in different parts of the world. Second, the teacher could introduce learners to archaeological research in communities in the United States. Third, the teacher might challenge class members to attempt their own lay archaeological investigations.

At the first stage, a good introductory source to convey some of the appeals, techniques, and contributions of archaeology is *The Past Is Human* by Peter White. The teacher could use excerpts such as these:

> Many people have always wanted to be archaeologists and they are quite right, it's a deal of fun for much of the time. ...

> ... In the last twenty years it is archaeologists who have proved that man has been alive for at least two and a half million years, that he was responsible for the cave art of France 10,000 to 25,000 years ago, and that about 10,000 years ago he invented the agriculture on which we still depend. It is the archaeologists who proved Homer and Beowulf were not simply stories by finding Troy and Sutton Hoo; it was they who finally proved that the Vikings discovered America in about A.D. 1000. Archaeology is wide open to new ideas, new theories about the past. Theories, not guesses.

> Archaeology is like a detective story. We may believe that the butler did it, but can we prove it? ...

> Garbage, trash, litter, rubbish and junk are all part of man's way of life. Wherever we go, we expect to find junk left by the people there before us. This may be as ordinary as the beer-cans and orange-peel left by a previous camper, as unusual as the scientific instruments an astronaut left on the moon, or as beautiful as the golden tomb of the Pharaoh Tutankhamun in Egypt. But in each case what we find is essentially junk—things left by their owners who either had no intention of recovering or recycling them or who never got around to doing so. Junk is the archaeologist's paradise.
> ... From (junk) we can reconstruct something of the lives of ordinary people, not only of priests and kings.

> ... Archaeological excavation is designed to make sense of jumbles of junk. This is why archaeologists spend so much time digging with trowels and dental picks, why there are so many photographs and drawings and notes ...

> ... If we listen, the garbage of the past speaks to us. [39]

Just in the past few years, there have been a number of books and articles concerned with important and even startling studies being carried out in various places in the world, which the teacher might report to learners and/or distribute to individual students for independent reading. For example, *People of the Lake: Mankind and Its Beginnings,* by Richard E. Leakey and Roger Lewin lists "an extraordinary wealth of discoveries" yielded "the past five years" by "sites scattered along the Rift Valley, in Tanzania, Kenya, and Ethiopia," including archaeologist Helène Roche's find of "stone tools which were struck around 2.5 million years ago, making them the oldest undisputed stone implements in the archaeological record." [40] "In Search of Atlantis" is an illustrated article from *Motorboat* , a magazine some students might like to thumb through for their enjoyment anyway. In 20 feet of water, off the coast of North Bimini is a site called the "Bimini road," which "stood on dry land 12,000 years ago," could have been "built by an advanced civilization in remote antiquity," and, according to Dr. David Zink, "may come to be recognized as the major archaeological discovery of the century in the New World."[41] In the "Archeology" section of the August 1978 issue of *Atlas World Press Review,* an article by Peter Baumann discusses the recent discovery of a civilization that flourished in Ecuador more than 5,000 years ago. This find "will dramatically alter perceptions of the origins of American civilizations." Baumann writes, "Another chapter in the history of mankind has been revealed."[42] And, *National Geographic* for April 1978 contains an article entitled "The First Emperor's Army: China's Incredible Find," which is illustrated generously. A caption for one of the pictures reads as follows:

> ... In 210 B.C. (Ch'in Shih Huang Ti) was buried under an earth mound 15 stories high called Mount Li. The site has long been recognized, but like many ancient tombs in China it has not yet been excavated. Recently, less than a mile from this mount, well diggers stumbled on a huge subterranean vault, a part of the grave complex. Now archaeologists are exploring its extraordinary treasure: the emperor's guardian army of 6,000 life-size pottery men and horses.[43]

The second stage in the approach suggested here is to increase learners' awareness of archaeological work in American communities. James Deetz is the author of an especially useful paperback, *In Small Things Forgotten: The Archaeology of Early American Life,* from which the teacher might read aloud. Deetz's seventh chapter, "Parting Ways," should be particulary interesting to students, and the teacher might share with her or his class selections such as these:

> The Parting Ways site (named for a fork in the road from Plymouth, Massachusetts to Plympton in one direction and Carver in the other) is but one of a number of sites, occupied by blacks in early America, now being investigated. In the years to come, Afro-American archaeology is certain to become an important and vital component of historical archaeology in the United States. Since the artifactual and architectural remains of these communities are a better index of the life of Afro-Americans in their own terms, they hold great promise of supplementing American black history in a different and important way. ...
>
> It was while (a) cellar was being excavated that a discovery was made that raised a number of important questions about the site and its inhabitants. Broken on the cellar floor were two large earthenware jars unlike any before encountered on a New England historical site. Eighteen inches tall, of red, unglazed, well-fired clay, their shape and physical characteristics immediately set them apart from the entire Anglo-American ceramic tradition. These jars were probably made in the West Indies; in their shape they are almost identical to pottery produced in West Africa. They are said to have been used at times for storing and shipping tamarind, a West African cultivated fruit that was grown in the West Indies. ... Their initial discovery at Parting Ways suggests that they might well relate to the African and West Indian background of the people who lived there. ... [44]

The third stage consists of motivating elementary and secondary learners to conduct their own amateur archaeological studies. This research might begin independently with a single artifact, progress to a small group study of, say, a limited collection of objects found in a box, barrel, or trunk, and culminate with excavation and/or observation in a larger context, such as an old junk pile, layer by layer from the top down. In any event, here are some imaginary titles of possible projects:

"A Rummage Sale at the Colonial Heights Presbyterian Church"
"My Great-Aunt Myrtle's Hope Chest"
"Garbage on the Beach Next to Catfish Lake"
"My Neighbor's Button Collection"
"A Storage Room at the Back of the Corn Bread County Pioneer Historical Museum"
"An Archaeological Dig—Top to Bottom—in the Big Drawer Under My Dad's Workbench"
"Looking for Stuff in the Abandoned Brickyard on the Edge of Town"
"The Excavation for the Metro Savings and Loan Company Building"
"A Shed behind My Uncle Neil's House"
"The Basements of Three Houses Pushed Down for Urban Renewal"
"Debris Found in the Ashes After the Acme Warehouse Fire"
"The Hole for the Public Swimming Pool"
"My Great-Grandmother Phinney's Walk-In Closet"
"Mr. Klemper Saves *Everything* in Egg Crates in His Garage!"

Conclusion

Culture is not only the key concept in anthropology and a substantial construct in the social sciences, but it is also one of the most important and potentially inspirational ideas for humankind to understand, contemplate, and apply, today and tomorrow.

Edward T. Hall, author of *The Silent Language* and *The Hidden Dimension*, underscores the importance of culture in this passage from *Beyond Culture:*

> There are two related crises in the world of contemporary man. The first and most visible is the population/environment crisis. The second, more subtle but equally lethal, is man himself—his relationship to himself, to his extensions, his institutions, his ideas, to those around him, as well as between the many groups that inhabit the globe; in a word, his relationship to his culture. [45]

In *The Gentle Tasaday: A Stone Age People in the Philippine Rain Forest,* John Nance expresses the inspirational potentiality of a comprehensive concept of culture:

> Yet even as we looked ahead, something in me lingered in the green heart of the Tasaday forest, where we had touched some kind of paradise—gentle people taking no more from nature than they needed each day, nibbling flowers, playing under the waterfall, laughing over *lassus,* weeping over good-bys, cuddling children, embracing friends, unashamedly expressing their love. Whatever lay ahead, that glimpse of Eden could not be denied. No matter how many centuries of history separated the Tasaday from us, whatever our world and their world would find in each other tomorrow, we had shared feelings and experiences that began a mutual history; that underscored our common humanity; that from their peace invited us to "call all men one man, and all women one woman." [46]

Surely elementary and secondary social studies teachers who make it possible for learners to gain a more meaningful understanding of the concept of culture and a heightened appreciation of "the psychic and cultural oneness of humankind," as Professor Pelto has expressed it, have earned another worthwhile piece of social immortality.

Notes

1. Margaret Mead, *Blackberry Winter: My Earlier Years* (New York: Pocket Books, 1975), p. 325.

2. Morris Freilich, ed., *The Meaning of Culture: A Reader in Cultural Anthrpology* (Lexington, Mass.: Xerox, 1972), p. vi.

3. Charles F. Keyes, *The Golden Peninsula: Culture and Adaptation in Mainland Southeast Asia* (New York: MacMillan Publishing Co., 1977). p. 9.

4. For example, see Adrian Cowell, *The Tribe That Hides from Man* (New York: Stein and Day, Publishers, 1974); Robert F. Gray, *The Sonjo of Tanganyika: An Anthropological Study of an Irrigation-Based Society* (Westport, Conn.: Greenwood Press, 1974); Farley Mowat, *The Siberians* (New York: Penguin Books, 1972); John Nance, *The Gentle Tasaday: A Stone Age People in the Philippine Rain Forest* (New York: Harcourt Brace Jovanovich, 1977); John Nyakatura, *Aspects of Bunyoro Customs and Tradition* (Nairobi, Kampala, Dar es Salaam: East African Literature Bureau, 1970); S. S. Sankan, *The Maasai* (Nairobi, Kampala, Dar es Salaam: East African Literature Bureau, 1971); Elizabeth Marshall Thomas, *Warrior Herdsmen* (New York: Vintage Books, 1972); Colin M. Turnbull, *The Mountain People* (New York: Simon and Schuster, 1972); and Thomas Rhys Williams, *The Dusun: A North Borneo Society* (New York: Holt, Rinehart and Winston, 1965).

5. Williams, *The Dusun*, p. 17.

6. E. B. White, *Charlotte's Web* (New York: Harper & Row, 1952), pp. 45-46. Excerpt from *Charlotte's Web* by E. B. White. Copyright, 1952, by E. B. White. By permission of Harper & Row, Publishers, Inc.

7. Rudyard Kipling, "Rikki-tikki-tavi" in *The Jungle Books* (New York: The New American Library, 1961), pp. 97-98.

8. Robert C. O'Brien, *Mrs. Frisby and the Rats of NIMH* (New York: Antheneum, 1971), pp. 159, 168, 170. Reprinted by permission of Atheneum Publishers from *Mrs. Frisby and the Rats of NIMH* by Robert C. O'Brien. Copyright © 1971 Robert C. O'Brien.

9. Richard Adams, *Watership Down* (New York: Macmillan Publishing Co., 1972), pp. 425-26.

10. Jean Craighead George, *Julie of the Wolves* (New York: Harper & Row, 1972), pp. 6, 38, 121.

11. Walt Morey, *Gentle Ben* (New York: E. P. Dutton & Co., 1965), pp. 148, 158. From *Gentle Ben* by Walt Morey. Copyright, ©, 1965 by Walt Morey. Reprinted by permission of the publisher, Elsvier-Dutton.

12. Allan W. Eckert, *Incident at Hawk's Hill* (Boston: Little, Brown and Co., 1971), pp. 154-55, 156-57, 182-83. Copyright © 1971 by Allan W. Eckert. By permission of Little, Brown and Co.

13. Jack London, *The Call of the Wild* and *White Fang* (New York: Macmillan, 1962), pp. 313-14, 317, and 323-24, respectively.

14. Goran Bergman, *Why Does Your Dog Do That?* (New York: Howell Book House, 1970).

15. For example, see Gordon Bermant, ed., *Perspectives on Animal Behavior* (Glenview, Ill.: Scott, Foresman and Co., 1973); Irenaus Eibl-Eibesfeldt, *Ethology: The Biology of Behavior* (New York: Holt, Rinehart and Winston, 1970); Heinz Friedrich, ed., *Man and Animal: Studies in Behavior* (New York: St. Martin's Press, 1972); Leonard A. Rosenblum, ed., *Primate Behavior: Developments in Field and Laboratory Research*, vol. 1 (New York: Academic Press, 1970); Allan M. Schrier, Harry F. Harlow, and Fred Stollnitz, eds., *Behavior of Nonhuman Primates: Modern Research Trends* (New York: Academic Press, 1965); John Paul Scott, *Animal Behavior*, 2d rev. ed. (Chicago: University of Chicago Press, 1972); and William N. Tavolga, *Principles of Animal Behavior* (New York: Harper & Row, 1969).

16. Kent Durden, *Gifts of an Eagle* (New York: Simon and Schuster, 1974), pp. 69, 77, 82.

17. Farley Mowat, *Never Cry Wolf* (Boston: Little, Brown and Co., 1965), pp. 68-70. Copyright © 1963 by Farley Mowat. By permission of Little, Brown and Co. in association with the Atlantic Monthly Press.

18. Jane van Lawick-Goodall, *In the Shadow of Man* (Boston: Houghton Mifflin Co., 1972), pp. 244-45.

19. Maurice K. Temerlin, *Lucy: Growing Up Human: A Chimpanzee Daughter in a Psychotherapist's Family* (Palo Alto, Calif.: Science and Behavior Books, 1977), pp. ix, 11, 106-7, 111 (Bantam Edition). By permission of the publisher.

20. Lanie Dills, *The 'Official' CB Slanguage Language Dictionary* (New York: Louis J. Martin & Associates, 1977), pp. 1, 10, 23, 26, 35, 46, 58, 61, 63, 69, 115.

21. Julia Child, Louisette Bertholle, and Simone Beck, "Sauces," in *Mastering the Art of French Cooking* (New York: Alfred A. Knopf, 1969), pp. 54-115.

22. Julia Child and Simone Beck, "Baking: Breads, Brioches, Croissants, and Pastries," in *Mastering the Art of French Cooking, vol. 2* (New York: Alfred A. Knopf, 1970), p. 58.

23. Wilfred Funk, *Word Origins and Their Romantic Stories* (New York: Grosset & Dunlap, 1950), p. 326.

24. The words used here have been selected from F. M. Kercheville, comp. "A Preliminary Glossary of New Mexican Spanish," in Carlos E. Cortes, ed. *Hispano Culture of New Mexico* (New York: Arno Press, 1976), pp. 59-67. Reprint of F. M. Kercheville, comp. "A Preliminary Glossary of New Mexican Spanish," *The University of New Mexico Bulletin* 5, no. 3 (15 July 1934): pp. 59-67.

25. Gilbert A. Jarvis, Therese M. Bonin, Donald E. Corbin, and Diane W. Birckbichler, *Vivent les differences* (New York: Holt, Rinehart and Winston, 1977), p. 166. [Italics mine.]

26. Verna Aardema, *Ji-Nongo-Nongo Means Riddles* (New York: Four Winds Press, 1978), pp. 10, 18, 22. From *Ji Nongo Nongo Means Riddles* by Verna Aardema, text copyright © 1978 by Verna Aardema. Reprinted by permission of Four Winds Press, a division of Scholastic Magazines, Inc.

27. Sankan, *The Maasai*, pp. 85-102.

28. Richard Lewis, collector, *Miracles: Poems by Children of the English-Speaking World* (New York: Simon and Schuster, 1966), pp. 26, 179. Copyright © 1966 by, Richard Lewis. Reprinted by permission of Simon & Schuster, a Division of Gulf & Western Corporation.

29. John Bierhorst, ed., *In the Trail of the Wind: American Indian Poems and Ritual Orations* (New York: Dell Publishing Co., 1975), p. 96.

30. Nyakatura, *Aspects of Bunyoro Customs and Traditions*, p. 113.

31. Mowat, *Never Cry Wolf*, pp. 89-90. Copyright © 1963 by Farley Mowat. By permission of Little, Brown and Co. in association with Atlantic Monthly Press.

32. Alfonso M. diNola, comp. and Patrick O'Connor, ed., *The Prayers of Man* (New York: Ivan Obolensky, 1961), pp. 13, 71, 86.

33. John J. Barsotti, annotator, *SCOOUWA: James Smith's Indian Captivity Narrative* (Columbus: Ohio Historical Society, 1978), pp. 7, 5.

34. *Ibid*, pp. 20, 24, 28, 29, 30, 31.

35. George M. Foster and Robert V. Kemper, eds., *Anthropologists in Cities* (Boston: Little, Brown and Co., 1974), p. 2.

36. I. M. Lewis, *Social Anthropology in Perspective: The Relevance of Social Anthropology* (New York: Penguin Books, 1976), p. 24.

37. Foster and Kemper, *Anthropologists in Cities*, pp. 1-2.

38. Susan W. Byrne, "Arden, an Adult Community," in George M. Foster and Robert V. Kemper, eds. *Anthropologists in Cities* (Boston: Little, Brown and Co., 1974), pp. 130, 132, 133.

39. Peter White, *The Past Is Human* (New York: Taplinger Publishing Co., 1976), pp. unnumbered, 2, 5, 11, 13. © 1974 by Peter White. Reprinted by permission.

40. Richard E. Leakey and Robert Lewin, *People of the Lake: Mankind and Its Beginnings* (Garden City, N. Y.: Anchor Press/Doubleday, 1978), pp. 17-18.

41. Reg Bragonier, "In Search of Atlantis," *Motorboat* 5, no. 6 (June 1978): 52-57.

42. Peter Baumann, "Man's Oldest Culture?," *Atlas World Press Review* 25, no. 8 (August 1978): 49.

43. Audrey Topping, "The First Emperor's Army: China's Incredible Find," *National Geographic* 153, no. 4 (April 1978): 440.

44. James Deetz, *In Small Things Forgotten: The Archaeology of Early American Life* (Garden City, N.Y.: Anchor Press/Doubleday, 1977), pp. 153-54, 147-49. Excerpted from *In Small Things Forgotten*, by James Deetz. Copyright © 1977 by James Deetz. Reprinted by permission of Doubleday and Company, Inc.

45. Edward T. Hall, *Beyond Culture* (Garden City, N.Y.: Anchor Books, 1977), p. 1.

46. Nance, *The Gentle Tasaday: A Stone Age People in the Philippine Rain Forest* (New York: Harcourt Brace Jovanovich, 1977), p. 451.

Index